The State University

The State University

Austin

Edited by Logan Wilson

Addresses Delivered at a Conference
Held in the Seventy-Fifth Year of
The University of Texas

University of Texas Press

Library of Congress Catalog Card No. 59–11720

© 1959 by the University of Texas Press

Published as a Supplement to *The Texas Quarterly*, Volume II, Number 2

First paperback printing, 2012

ISBN : 978-0-292-74200-0

Contents

Introduction

THE CONFERENCE on issues confronting the state university, held at the University of Texas in November 1958, was part of the University's celebration of its seventy-fifth year. Like all other events in that celebration, the conference was designed to mark new routes in the future rather than to memorialize the past.

Other anniversary activities in Texas, focused on the belief that the state university is not only an institution important in American history but also a center of influence upon the nation's future, provided a background for this conference. Seventy-five leading citizens of Texas accepted membership in a committee charged by the Board of Regents to consider the University's present state and its development during the next twenty-five years. The Report of the Committee of Seventy-Five was a document distinguished equally for the generosity and public spirit with which these citizens gave themselves and their time to its making, for the frankness and courage with which they confronted immediate facts, and for the resolute determination with which they put their main conclusion: that the University of Texas should move forward, steadily and realistically, toward eminence. This Report, distributed at the turn of the seventy-sixth year, has been considered at length by the Regents. It is now being put into action.

The Committee on Expectations, composed of other leading citizens, members of the faculty of the Main University, and representatives of the student body, has made a similar study of the University at Austin. Conferences, administrative studies, and a carefully planned series of lectures have supplemented the work of these two major committees.

Most significant to American education in general were the discussions for which the following addresses provided the basis. Seventy-three members of the administrations and faculties of other American universities joined in the conference. A full report of the proceedings will be issued later. Meanwhile, the principal addresses stand both as definition of the present context of institutions like the University of Texas and as prophecy of the problems and opportunities which all such universities face in the near future of the United States. This note of prophecy has been sounded by L. D. Haskew, Vice-President for Developmental Services, who was in charge of all activities of the Seventy-Fifth Year:

The Seventy-Fifth Year closed on January 9, 1959; but it is not yet history. Essentially, it is a combination of direction and motive power which will work itself out in history. Its outcomes can never be measured. In its own right, the Seventy-Fifth Year was never very important. The important thing is to move a great university toward eminence.

Moving steadily toward that goal, the University of Texas recognizes its share in the common lot of higher education in the United States. It acknowledges its growing debt to the whole company of scholars who have made the American university an ideal and a fact, and to free citizens everywhere who have advanced the cause of knowledge. Keenly aware of its immediate and local responsibility, it willingly assumes a great obligation—the common cause of all free institutions.

The State University

The University's Relationships with Other Colleges and Universities

By David D. Henry

I

President Buchanan's message with the veto of the first Land-Grant Act approved by the Congress reflected not only the doubt and skepticism which assailed the uncertain beginnings of the institutions for "agriculture and the mechanic arts"; it also showed the concern of other institutions over the development of public universities in general.

After the Land-Grant Act was finally approved, over the exceedingly vocal opposition of the nongovernment educational institutions, criticism continued at the state level. Existing institutions vied among one another for the federal grant. Communities competed for the location of the new institution. Some institutions and some communities opposed acceptance of the grants.

Nearly every state university at one time or another has been beset with criticism, opposition, or misunderstanding, both from nongovernment institutions and from other public institutions.

The fact that the comprehensive state university has grown in scope and strength should not lead to complacency, to thinking that the critics have been dispersed, that debate on fundamental issues can be avoided, or that institutional relations can be ignored.

We may discount the current talk about asking the student to pay the full cost of his education as inconsistent with the tradition of the people's university, one available to all who have the ability to meet its requirements. We may minimize the current talk about limiting enrollments to those who are exceptionally talented as being inconsistent with the American dream of education for all who can profit from educational service. We may believe that the current talk about ceiling on expenditures for education is inconsistent with the studies that show that the state universities have been responsible for improvements in the economy far beyond any expenditures made upon them, improvements arising from new knowledge, from trained personnel, and from implementation of new ideas. But these topics are receiving serious public attention and they are but representative of a number of others to which the state universities must aggressively respond.

(Throughout the remainder of this paper as an abbreviated reference the phrase "the state university" will be used to describe a comprehensive state university, organized to serve the state as a whole without limitation in function, in scope, or in geographic area.)

I mention past and present criticisms as a prelude to a consideration of the state university's relationship to other colleges and universities because an intelligent long-range positive program to gain wide public understanding must take them into account; and the public understanding of the state university is markedly influenced by what the presidents, faculties, and trustees of other colleges and universities say on these subjects. The public atmosphere in which the fundamental conditions for future growth are determined may be beclouded or cleared by the reactions of institutional neighbors.

On this point, I am sure that all of us have at times been baffled and perplexed, sometimes dismayed, by the nature of the comment of representatives of other institutions. All of us could produce public statements of educators in responsible positions critical of other institutions generically or individually, statements not only in exceedingly bad taste, bordering on the unprofessional in unvalidated and unscholarly negative comment, but also dangerous to the welfare of higher education in confusing the public as to the needs and opportunities of institutions.

We should have a code of professional conduct which would deal harshly with such behavior. Institutions must be held accountable, and their critics should speak their minds. But criticism should be accurate, substantiated, and voiced with professional restraint and understanding.

I would not deal with institutional relations merely as a part of a strategy for improved public support, however. Incumbent upon all state universities is the expectation for educational statesmanship in working for a prudent and wise utilization of a state's resources, for leadership in planning for maximum results from the expenditures of the state's educational dollars and energy. Institutional relations obviously condition probable success in fulfilling these responsibilities.

It is appropriate, then, that a view of the future of the state university should begin with a consideration of relationships with other institutions.

II

The fundamental issues in relationships among the institutions of the state come into view in a consideration of state planning, both for long range and immediate problems. It is not enough for the state university to measure its institutional relations through the activities of the office of admissions, arrangements for transfer students, the amenities of a scholarship program, personnel exchange practices, or occasional conferences. These are all important but they do not substitute for initiative in building machinery for sound educational planning for a state.

At this point, it is well to emphasize the importance of state planning in general. In the widespread new concern about the welfare of higher education, the average citizen is ambivalent in his attitude toward the tasks ahead. On the one hand, he is amazed at the projected cost in dollars and energy to gear up the educational enterprise to the requirements of the space age. On the other hand, he realizes that education has now become an instrument of national defense and international policy as well as of economic strength and individual fulfillment. He knows that he must support it adequately.

As he studies ways and means to strengthen education, Mr. Average Citizen expects wise planning, prudent management, and efficient utilization of educational resources. He is beginning to ask for state planning as a condition for greater support. Unilateral, institutional expansion without professional study of the needs of the state as a whole or of the potential contribution of all institutions supplying that need, public and private, will appear to him unwise. Favoring one geographical area at the expense of another will not make much sense. He will expect new developments to be based on a broad view of higher education in the public service, upon facts rather than bias, upon consultation rather than competition, and upon the ability to evolve adequate machinery for the implementation of interinstitutional action.

What are the responsibilities of the state university in state planning?

Some say, "Why bother about what others do? Why not chart one's own course, go his own way?" A ready answer, already suggested, is that participation in state planning is a matter of intelligent self-interest. Obviously, what happens in any one institution affects in some way every institution. For example, no state university can ignore the impact upon its own work from the efforts of regional institutions to undertake statewide responsibilities. No state university can ignore the development of junior colleges. No state university can ignore the expansion of other institutions within the state and remain efficient or realistic in its own programming.

More important, however, is the public view of the state university as having a responsibility to the state as a whole on many fronts. In the record of many state universities it is clear that the people have expected them to exercise leadership in the planning of all subjects related to the state's welfare where education and research have a bearing.

Beyond current necessity and historical expectation for state university participation in state planning, there is the inherent professional obligation to have the university's resources utilized in the improvement of education service in general.

Accepting these premises for the state university's role in state planning, one then asks, how is it appropriately expressed?

Here, times have changed. At one time in a number of instances the views of the state university were dominant in educational planning, both in influence upon the secondary schools and elementary schools and upon other institutions. It is something of an understatement to say that today the views of the state university are not dominant; in fact, very often they are not sought. It is now possible for a nationally known consultant on a state problem in higher education to render a public report upon an important new development and have that report receive serious public consideration although no one at the state university was asked to contribute to it or comment upon it.

What has happened in the past twenty-five to fifty years to bring this change?

Obviously, as other institutions have become stronger they have come to be important factors in a state's program. Tensions have developed not only among public and private institutions but among the public institutions. Competition for the available state dollar has grown. The growth of regional institutions has encouraged geographical alignments. The concern of nongovernment institutions about what appears to be the enlarged absorptive capacity of the state university has made them fearful of their own prospects. Careless or indifferent administration has on occasion contributed to misunderstandings.

President J. L. Morrill raised the issue pointedly in his address to the National Association of State Universities on May 5, 1958. He said,

It seems to me quite clear that the history and development of public higher education in this country have conceded the pre-eminence of the comprehensive state university and the combined state and land-grant institution. And I would raise the question as to whether that pre-eminence is endangered and imperiled in the currently changing higher educational scene in a good many states, with the later prospect of more of the same in other states.

Mr. Morrill concluded with this statement:

It seems to me inevitable that there will be what one might characterize as a horizontal dispersion of educational opportunity in our states at the lower liberal arts, teacher-training, pre-professional levels—but that a vertical divisibility of our higher level and more comprehensive function in science and scholarship and research, so long and arduously achieved, would be a calamity of public policy and educational effectiveness.

While we may believe that state planning is inevitable and that sound state planning may indeed result in conserving the traditional role of the state university, in encouraging a prudent use of the state's resources, and in restoring an orderly pattern where there is now confusion of relationships, we must also take note of the parallel public concern with the question of enforced coordination of the state universities and other institutions. The new interest in this subject arises from different sources, for different reasons: from some who have an interest in making sure that sound state planning will be quickly effective; from others who have an interest only in limiting expenditures.

A single board of control for the public institutions within a state is not a panacea, however. Experience with this mechanism is uneven among the states where it has been tried and at best it cannot deal adequately with the institutions outside its jurisdiction. Further, merely amalgamating boards of control or creating a "super board" does not automatically achieve the result desired among the institutions directly concerned. In the more complex situations, particularly, there should also be carefully designed plans for integration of administration and of program and agreement on general objectives. Without such integration, a super-board plan may but transfer present confusion from one arena to another.

There are those who say that voluntary planning, without any new machinery, is enough. Unfortunately, the record on voluntary planning is not very good. There are a few examples in the United States where such planning is apparently working. However, one institution moving in a competitive spirit and without regard for the welfare of the state as a whole, one "empire builder," can destroy cooperative relationships. In such a situation, the state university cannot adequately make its case or reply to covert criticism because public quarrel is an inappropriate posture for a professionally responsible agency.

The machinery for state planning cannot be patterned on example. Examples are always illustrative, but they do not prove. It is well to remember the limitations on comparisons. No two institutions can be compared, for they are unlike in too many ways. Nor can one state solve its problems by imitating others.

Institutions are like people. They resemble one another in many ways, but in personality, nature, temperament, purposes, character, each is an individual and must be understood as an individual.

States, too, must work out their problems in the light of their resources, their history, their standards and aspirations.

In trying to build a state plan for the future of higher education, there is not one answer but many. Junior colleges must be encouraged. Private institutions must be utilized to the utmost. New institutions may have to be established. Existing institutions must be helped to grow, expand, and develop.

In facing these new developments, moreover, it must be emphasized that coordination is a result, not a process. It cannot be imposed. It does not arrive suddenly. It does not come through edict or mandate. Effective state plans grow out of the experience of institutions in working together.

Institutional relationships must be hammered out in ways indigenous to a state community. The organization of one state may look effective, but still be ineffective in another. Coordination at the state level must take into account historical relationships and present capacities, as well as the intangibles of leadership.

There is little advantage to talking about planning, however, and enumerating the agenda unless there is "brass tacks" thinking about the mechanism to bring institutions together for the purposes here outlined. Voluntary meetings will not suffice when general interest lags or when one or more members are indifferent or hostile. Machinery for debate, for communication, and for appraisal must be formally instituted and used.

Sometimes that machinery will be general in nature, with broad purposes, illustrated by the Illinois Commission of Higher Education. Sometimes it will be specialized, starting with one problem, or a few, but having the potential to grow in scope and usefulness.

The important outcome of any consideration of this question is the creation of some continuing "ways and means" for joint consultation and action, however limited initially.

At this point it may be well to point out that while state planning may well begin with a state survey, it does not end there.

President J. Wayne Reitz of the University of Florida, in referring to "a rash of surveys at the state level of higher education," called attention to their overemphasizing the quantitative aspects of institutional service, their failure to take into account the informed evaluations of responsible administrators and lay leaders, their search for simplified answers to the need for coordination, with too much faith in "super boards" and superimposed chancellors, their failure to take proper cognizance of varying institutional objectives and responsibilities.

In the end, the effectiveness of state planning rests with the willingness of the individual institutions to participate and with the desire on the part of each to work with others in the attack on larger problems. Such willingness and desire will be expressed only when there is no threat, direct or indirect, to the institution's autonomy or individuality, when there is no possibility of regimentation or political force. "The objective," says the Educational Policies Commission in its 1957 report, "should be maximum voluntary cooperation, arrived at by continuing study and supported by whatever framework of agreement is advantageous." All efforts at coordination, the Report continues, "must in the end depend upon the action of individual institutions—action based upon voluntary judgment, action designed to preserve the individuality of the institution within the pattern of the whole American enterprise."

In the presence of these imponderables, what course shall the state university take?

The state university, by its tradition, by its present role, by its future opportunity, by its inherent responsibility, has a duty to support state planning and to give leadership to improved institutional relationships. It should work for the establishment of machinery to facilitate inter-institutional consultation and cooperation. Its standards in institutional behavior should be the highest; its practices in institutional relations the best. The university is a pace-setter here as in other educational endeavor. In no other way can it fulfill its leadership role.

No institution should regard what is best for the state as a whole as in any way inimical to its own development.

To exemplify its attitude on state planning and to encourage the approach here advocated, the state university should be willing to have all plans, including its own, submitted to impartial scrutiny along the following lines:

1. The specific need for a proposed new program should be defined.
2. Plans to fill the need for a new program should not be adopted until ways and means to fulfill existing needs in the same field for which the state already has an obligation are measured.
3. Further, new major obligations should not be undertaken until existing needs in all fields in all institutions are examined and priorities considered.
4. Then, proposed new programs at all institutions should be considered, to see if any have equal or prior claim upon the state's resources.
5. Finally, consideration should be given to the problem when, where, and how the specific need upon which the proposal is based may best be fulfilled.

With restraint in answering unfair criticism, with patience in dealing with unwise demands, with objectivity in viewing the needs of the commonwealth, the state university must persevere in leading the way for improved institutional relationships in general and for state planning in particular; it must press for the creation of appropriate machinery to give statewide appraisal to professionally prepared and objectively considered recommendations.

The way is uncharted and intricate. How to get the best in planning without having the planners take over the professional responsibilities of the universities is a central question in the future of interinstitutional relations.

III

Significant progress will come in the improvement of institutional relations and in the evolution of effective ways and means for state planning only if there are some commonly accepted premises—premises accepted within the state university, by the public, and by the other institutions involved. Without such broad acceptance, progress will be spotty and the attainment of the ultimate goal of coordinated growth for maximum effectiveness by all institutions will be impossible—whether institutional relations are organized by voluntary planning, by imposed statewide management, or by some moderate way in between the two methods.

The premises are these:

1. The welfare of higher education is indivisible. What helps one, in basic strength, helps all. What helps the group or hurts it, helps or hurts each one in some measure.

Tensions have too often developed from the mistaken notion that there is a single pot of money for education for which each institution must compete in a way that a larger share for one means less for someone else, or that there is a limited number of students. While this may be true at any one time, in a given situation, in the long run there is more to do than all put together will get done. Further, there are enough resources to go around if higher education as a totality makes sufficient impact upon the public mind.

Acceptance of this point of view will do much to ease interinstitutional tensions and make possible the united approach to greater achievements on behalf of all of higher education.

2. We shall not make as much progress as we should in state or regional planning unless the spirit of inquiry is upon the individual institutions. Each institution should be clear as to its achievements, its resources, its objectives. Intramural planning is a condition of effective interinstitutional relations on a state or regional basis. Mutual regard and respect among institutions are impossible without it. External understanding depends upon internal clarification.

3. Choices must be made by each institution, and neighboring institutions must know of them. Under the pressure of additional numbers and many other new demands, with resources limited in any one period, the university today must make choices. It cannot be all things to all people and maintain quality and over-all effectiveness.

The state university historically has accepted the assumption that it would be not only a comprehensive instructional institution for college-age youth but also a service institution, willing to do anything of educational good for the general public.

This premise may have been acceptable at a time when there were a limited number of agencies for higher education and related services; but today, in the interest of efficiency and quality and the best utilization of future resources, the state university must make some choices.

Similarly, a state will have to determine if it prefers the strength that comes from the consolidation of specialized educational resources, or by what other method to allocate function and relate institutional responsibility to resources available.

While these premises are essential for orderly progress in institutional relations, some popular myths have to be eliminated to make them effective. Representatives of the institutional neighbors of state universities should help to destroy these false notions.

The idea that quantity and quality are opposites is such a myth. The fear of institutional size is unreasoned and overdrawn.

Quality is a matter of resources and purpose, not of size. It is derived from standards, not from numbers. It is influenced by people, not statistics. The large institution devoted to standards, determined to have quality, insistent upon achievement by students and teachers in the classroom, upon the best of personnel practices and the highest qualifications in professional selection, will have quality if it has resources. The smallest institution with the smallest teacher-pupil ratio without these standards will not have quality.

The only size that is important to the individual is the size of the group or the groups of which he is a member.

The large university with a balanced program—that is, balance between number of lower division and advanced students, among professional offerings, among activities in instruction, research, and service —such a university with resources enough to do its job has no reason to be concerned about its size.

Growth is a normal function of a living institution. To stimulate growth artificially is unwise. To promote growth indiscriminately is unsound. To limit growth arbitrarily is likewise unwise and unsound. However, to plan for the university's growth to be in balance with respect to its several responsibilities and in relationship to its resources is a primary obligation of all concerned with its administration.

The ultimate size of a university is beyond definition, and the arithmetic is not significant. As long as the university has the resources to do its work and keeps a proper balance within the objectives outlined, with quality of performance a controlling objective, it will continue to increase in strength and stature and effectiveness. Size, under such conditions, may be a virtue, not a subject for apology.

Another popular myth is that there is a ceiling on educational growth —that a limitation on resources inevitably drives us in the direction of an educational elite.

When we look at the total resources of any state and the nation and both public and private support for higher education, at the percentage of the total national income spent on higher education in comparison with that applicable to other expenditures on which the American public puts a high premium, we may conclude that only a partial contribution to higher education has been made in comparison with what can be done and needs to be done.

Another myth confronting the comprehensive state university is that education service should be regionalized.

If we consider the state as a community and arrange each service for the best interest of the state as a whole, the location of the service is unimportant. The regional concept in distribution of state service is not only an anachronism; it leads to inefficient dividing up of state services and often invites purely political arrangements. In the modern age of transportation, it is obvious that the regional factor is significant mainly when the institution serves students who must live at home while going to school.

Other topics on which there are false notions which should be cleared away are:

1. Voluntary giving to state universities
2. The nature of public control in relation to institutional integrity
3. Admission policies and practices
4. Charges to students
5. Curricular quality and emphases
6. Public education in a free enterprise economy
7. The quality of management and administration
8. The moral and spiritual quality of faculty and student personnel

If these premises are not accepted and the myths destroyed, then institutional relationships will have to be umpired by an outside agency or controls imposed by an outside authority. On the other hand, the way is still open in most states for cooperation in the evolution of state planning as a basis for improved institutional relationships, or for improved relationships as a basis for improved state planning, whichever objective is of immediate concern. The urgency of the need for progress on this front and the intensity of the public interest in the general subject require now that we go beyond polite interest in what the other institutions are doing. Nor is it enough that each carry on its own planning, however creative or imaginative.

The best of intentions, the best internal planning, the most professional approach will be limited unless it is adequately communicated to the faculties and trustees and leaders of other colleges and universities. Further, there must even be a willingness to undertake joint action where such a course is indicated—an approach in which universities in general have not been very imaginative.

Communication before the fact is of the greatest importance. Communication before new plans are inaugurated when they affect other institutions is essential to the good faith and the utilization of ideas of others as to what is good for the state as a whole. Cooperative planning has shallow significance when advice is not sought at a time when it can be influential in the final decision. Basic to all cooperative planning is evidence of faith in mutual interest.

The report of the President's Committee on Education Beyond the High School has pointed up the total challenge on these issues: The "random approach" to public service "may have been sufficient when the need was far less complicated and urgent, but it is wholly inadequate for the individual and social needs of today and tomorrow."

"Planning now," the Report continues,

should be broad, built on national, regional, state and local needs; it should be comprehensive, involving all institutions and all agencies, resulting in "integrated or interrelated, flexible action programs"; it should include participation by laymen, both for their contributions and as a means of gaining their interest and support; and it should be based upon adequate information, although "action cannot always await complete study."

The Committee emphasizes that future planning activity will call for a higher degree of concentration, of sophistication, of mutual respect among the various agencies which provide education beyond the high school, and of mutual understanding and confidence between education and the society it serves, than has been typical in the past. Cooperative planning will do much to offset the dangers of complacency, traditionalism and provincialism.

Again to quote President Morrill,

Relations with Other Colleges and Universities

We are confronted, I think, with the *noblesse oblige* of a new and disinterested statesmanship in cooperation and consultation with all the colleges and universities of our state, private and public. . . . More than any other, we are the people's most productive investment in their own future—established, supported and controlled by the public that we serve.

The new developments in planning, arising from citizen concern with the financial requirements and the effectiveness of education, to be productive must be based upon a broad view of higher education in the public service, upon facts rather than custom or bias, upon consultation rather than competition, and upon the ability to evolve adequate machinery for interinstitutional cooperation. These are the factors in the pattern of institutional relations of the future.

Education for Undergraduates

By Charles E. Odegaard

The state university faces important issues today in the area of undergraduate education. There are a variety of problems which might be singled out. The first one to which I shall turn appears now with reference to almost all kinds of undergraduate education, but I shall come to it first from a direction with which I am very familiar because of my own history. Having been until recently a dean of arts and sciences, I shall begin by approaching our problem from the place of the under-graduate liberal arts college within the state university. A fundamentally important fact about the arts college in a state university is that charac-teristically there is superimposed upon it in the university structure a graduate school and a varying collection of graduate professional schools; and there are placed adjacent to it undergraduate professional schools. The undergraduate arts college in the typical state university thus operates in an environment very different from that of the so-called

18 ·

independent liberal arts college. The total environment of the state university constitutes both a problem for the undergraduate college and an opportunity. It requires considerable conscious planning and ingenuity to turn this size and variety from the possible disadvantage of cross purposes and confusion to the equally possible advantage of great enrichment and awareness of the manifold world about one.

In most state universities (as well as in many private institutions, which are similarly organized as complex educational structures), to the faculties of arts and sciences, undergraduate and graduate instruction are interrelated parts of a single burden. A large portion of the arts and sciences faculty is usually enmeshed in both levels of education at the same time. During the past century a characteristic feature in the life of the liberal arts college has been the push upward toward graduate education and the involvement of the faculty increasingly in research for that new knowledge which nourishes graduate teaching and makes the faculty man not only a maintainer of knowledge but also an advancer of knowledge. The push in the direction of research has created an internal tension and conflict among the demands of the teaching situation at successive levels, ranging from the awakening of the curiosity of entering freshmen to the critical evaluation of the doctoral dissertation of the Ph.D. aborning. While there are a few disciplines among the arts and sciences, usually rank newcomers to the fold, which are introduced to university students only in the higher reaches of undergraduate or even graduate years, representatives of most disciplines find themselves confronted with students at all successive levels over the seven- to ten-year span involved in a bachelor's and doctor's program.

Should one and the same faculty be vested with responsibilities for instruction over this entire span? In most state universities one and the same group of men in the arts and sciences provide both undergraduate and graduate instruction. There are teaching fellows and instructors who teach undergraduates only, but if they persevere, survive the apprenticeship period, and are retained and then possibly promoted, most of them acquire by some baptismal procedure an additional license, admission to the status of graduate faculty, which permits them to cut back an undergraduate course or two in order to find time also for graduate courses.

Whatever the outward appearance of things, there are real issues here. Serious imbalances can develop within one and the same institution in the degree to which the responsibilities of the faculty to undergraduate and graduate education are acquitted. Some departments may be composed of individuals who tend to shortchange undergraduates in time, attention, and imaginative teaching in favor of the graduate program. Other departments may reverse the balance and conduct an inadequate graduate program, undernourished because of insufficient original and critical work by the faculty. Still other departments may come closer to a harmonious balance by spreading their sense of responsibility and their responsible actions more evenly over the full range of their obligations to students, undergraduate and graduate.

There is no doubt that it is a bit of a trick to structure the growth of a department or a faculty so that it does a good, first-class job of instruction on all laps of this seven- to ten-year sprint. Over the years involved in a bachelor's and doctor's program, students change in maturity, in the accumulation of competence, and in motivation. Granted that there are individual variations among them, present practice as well as economy requires us to group students in categories rather than to conduct individual tutorials throughout this time sequence. Students do become packaged into freshmen receiving their first initiation into a discipline or an area of related disciplines, upperclassmen working on courses suitable for a major, and graduate students specializing toward a Ph.D. and finally writing a thesis. These students present very different kinds of instructional problems and situations to the faculty, and individual faculty members themselves vary in turn in their enthusiasm for these different levels and types of teaching.

What I am saying is obvious, but its full import is often not adequately grasped, especially at the level of action. Faculty members are human people operating in a social situation, and however individualistic they may tend to be, it is still in a relative sense, and they do not escape the social character of the human animal. It makes a world of difference in their objectives in teaching, and in the way in which they serve them, if there is a clearly perceived understanding of the responsibilities of the group to which they are admitted, shared at least by most of the faculty and their administrative colleagues. It seems to me highly desirable for an institution to try to develop internally a clear understanding of the over-all criteria which are appropriate to the goals and responsibilities of the academic group, and to apply them systematically and carefully at those decision points which affect the careers of the individual participants. The qualities sought for in recruiting new staff and in recommending original appointments should be clearly derived from these criteria. The basis of evaluation of the services of faculty and of recognition of them through promotion in rank and improvement in salary should be derived from these criteria. The philosophy which guides the nature and distribution from year to year of the assignments individual faculty members are asked to carry should coincide with the criteria, for by doing consistently the tasks of the role, men become more proficient in the role and more aware of its requirements. The criteria established need not mean an absolute uniformity of characteristics in all persons. They can be set so as to seek complementary virtues within the staff, with certain persons recognized for a high quality of performance in certain areas balanced by other persons recognized for a high quality of performance in other areas.

In short, there should be a personnel policy, each part of which is consistent with the established criteria for the group. It is not easy to achieve a clear description of the taxonomy of *homo academicus* because of the internal structure of universities and the way they work. Far more than consistent and grandiloquent pronouncements by deans and presidents are required. There must be consistent policy behind innumerable decisions at the department, school or college, and university levels. From the actions and advice of the circle of influential senior members of the faculty whose attitudes and behavior so largely determine the model to which the juniors will try to conform, there should emerge the outline of an accepted model consistent with the professional aims and obligations of the group. One of the most challenging tasks confronting chairmen of departments, deans, and presidents is to provide the imaginative and persistent leadership required to bring about within a large, varied, and individualistic group a common understanding of the basic rules of the road for faculty status and the means of implementation thereof. One need only listen to the conversation in the faculty club about appointments and promotions, and the arguments over the weight given to this or that activity, to realize that a satisfactory solution of this problem is hard to find.

Since the undergraduate arts college in a state university normally confronts graduate education as well, there is an issue in deciding how to group responsibilities for different kinds of instruction and the individuals who provide them. Should the individuals who offer instruction at all levels in a given discipline be grouped together in one department within one faculty of arts and sciences, thus retaining the more customary unitary faculty of arts and sciences responsible for both undergraduate and graduate education? Have arts and sciences faculties become so preoccupied with graduate education, its attendant specialization, and the commitment to research that they have lost a perspective, especially upon the general education usually associated with the explorations of underclass years? Should they accordingly be relieved of responsibility for these earlier years in favor of a separate underclass "college" faculty as in the University of Chicago experiment? Such experiments in administrative regroupings of faculties have at least the virtue of open recognition of a real problem in the definition and the allocation of responsibility for an important aspect of undergraduate teaching which is too often treated cavalierly in the specialist-oriented, graduate-dominated, unitary faculty of arts and sciences.

There is no doubt in my mind that the general education movement of the last twenty years has been a justifiable protest against the extremes of specialization. There is probably some justification also for the common tendency to regard the independent liberal arts college as being less afflicted by this weakness than the liberal arts college in a university, public or private. But I see no reason why this must necessarily be the case, providing the faculty of arts and sciences in a university really wants to vindicate its claim to offer a good undergraduate education as well as a good graduate program. Such a faculty may be exposed more directly to the hazards of close association with graduate education, but there are instances of strenuous efforts being made within state universities to provide improved undergraduate education. The matter of organization of the faculty and the clarification of objectives and responsibilities of members of the group take on real importance when one asks how a good job in both undergraduate and graduate education may be achieved in the complex university setting characteristic of our major state universities.

Since institutions vary, the organization suitable for one may not apply so well to another. Even so, I suppose we each have our prejudices —at least, I have mine. I have a preference for the unitary organization, in which, apart from the junior members who are undergoing an apprenticeship before they are admitted to the privilege of graduate teaching, practically all members of the college, and of the departments thereof, share responsibility for both undergraduate and graduate instruction. Any attempt to keep these two in tandem within one and the same group is fraught, I admit, with difficulties.

While I have had in mind in the foregoing statements especially the undergraduate program in arts and sciences, the same issue is arising increasingly in undergraduate professional colleges in which the emphasis upon the inculcation of professional practice is being supplemented by a growing interest in a basic science approach, in research, and in programs associated with more advanced degrees. Engineering in its various branches, business administration, pharmacy, nursing, forestry, fisheries, are all moving in directions which will expose them to the same pressures which have long been felt by arts and sciences faculties, and they will encounter similar problems.

To turn to a somewhat different set of problems, the existence in the state university of a number of schools or colleges giving a wide variety of undergraduate degree programs of instruction raises an issue with regard to the handling of what I often hear called "service" courses. I mean the courses which are offered for students who are enrolled not in the degree program for which the instructor's faculty is primarily organized but in a degree program sponsored by some other faculty. Because of the tendency, probably the increasing tendency, of professional schools to incorporate work in basic sciences and arts in their degree programs, the college of arts and sciences is likely to be the largest "service" unit on the campus. It may be more blessed to give than to receive, but the giver is also peculiarly exposed to the complaints of dissatisfied customers. One often hears the comment that chemistry is chemistry is chemistry, or English is English is English. So why should there be a dozen courses, each tailored to students from different schools on the campus? Let them all take the same course.

Economy, ease of organization for the professor, and the unity of the subject may argue for this, but the variations in previous background, ability levels, interest, and motivation among different school or college constituencies on a university campus warrant, in my judgment, a degree of recognition in planning service courses. The research orientation on a state university campus leads all too easily into indifference toward, or a lack of sympathy for, service courses and the students interested in them. Yet there is no better opportunity in our complex and highly differentiated culture by which to encourage a degree of mutual tolerance and respect among the various professions and careers than in the service-course portion of the operation of the schools and colleges of the university. The very conflict among faculty members from different units of the university over service courses for students can lead to mutual educational experiences among faculties. Arguments over humble service courses in universities torn apart by specialisms may help us recapture the idea of a university seeking ultimately that truth which is one.

The very diversity of undergraduate programs so characteristic of the state university, while it presents a rich array of possibilities for the student, also poses a problem to which I feel our institutions have not yet devoted enough attention. The entering freshman usually faces a bewildering battery of curriculums and courses. The universe is a big and varied place and I do not question the desirability of maintaining a rich variety of curriculums in our state universities. But how far should the university go in advising or counseling students through this maze so that they make some effort to try out their yet undiscovered capacities and end up pursuing courses for which they seem well suited? Should they be left by the university to "shop around" without benefit of a well-established, university-devised advisory system, dependent upon trial and error—or rather taste and distaste for the courses which they happened to take first—supplemented by what they obtain in free advice from fraternity brothers, campus-wise seniors, and chance faculty contact? Should there be then a university-sponsored advising system? If so, at what points and for what questions should the advising system be used? Who should man it? "Professional" counselors, part-time academic counselors, or faculty without any special allocation of time for this function? Can anything be done to simplify the induction process for the freshman? Does the array have to be quite so varied? Or is it in fact not so varied as appears on the surface, because the alternatives could, with more thought and systematic interpretation by the faculty, be presented to the freshmen in a less bewildering manner? I do not have very many firm answers to these questions. I do not believe that faculties have yet studied this part of the university operation enough to have final answers. This whole area tends to suffer from a kind of general neglect, relieved here and there by the struggles of a dedicated few, who run a real risk in terms of ultimate preferment by working on, and thinking about, aspects of the academic institution which are normally not thought about by many of their colleagues.

The presence within the state university of a graduate school and of various advanced professional schools may pose problems for undergraduate education, but it also gives opportunities for the development of a distinctive role in undergraduate education. While many kinds of service, many kinds of talent, are needed in our society, state universities are not necessarily places to train all skills and talents. Historically, they have developed the resources needed to serve as a special training ground for men and women possessed of more than ordinary powers in abstract thinking, quantitative and verbal. I mean by this, persons who have the ability mentally to keep several balls in the air; to see with the mind's eye turns down the road; to speculate about things; to detect that things are not always as they seem at first; to find behind the mystifying variety of fact consistencies, uniformities, patterns; to deal with the world at long range. In the very nature of the case, the kinds of mental work and the kinds of skills developed through disciplined use by graduate students and students of the advanced professions require this intellectual capacity beyond the ordinary. These students emerge inevitably as a highly selected group who have learned to discipline relatively unusual talent. They can become models for the younger undergraduates, awakening the interests of the latter and stimulating them to emulation. The very environment with which the advanced students must be surrounded to do their work, their libraries and laboratories, can serve to awaken the interest of undergraduates. Whatever else they may be, state universities with their graduate and professional schools should be peculiarly well suited to the education of the academically superior undergraduates who can be expected in time to become graduate and advanced professional students. Not to provide a program of instruction suitable for superior students is to waste an opportunity inherently present in the environment of a state university.

Yet we are singularly reluctant in this country to recognize differences in ability levels and to gear our instructional procedures accordingly. We accept differences in strength or athletic powers. We are not upset by recognition of the fact that musical or artistic talent has been distributed by an uneven hand. But it is somehow thought undemocratic to note that intellectual power, capacity for abstract thinking, is not rationed out evenly by the Creator. Yet are there not obvious differences among individuals on this score too?

These differences in capacities take on altered importance in various cultural settings. In the disorganized, tumultuous time of the Middle Ages, sheer physical prowess trained and disciplined for fighting, first on foot and then on horseback, was an important ingredient in leadership in a feudal society. Pandulf Ironhead obviously possessed certain requirements for survival and leadership in his era. In the complex, differentiated, interrelated, and highly organized society of our own time, there is an inevitable premium on talent, not for slugging, but for thinking, one's way through the intricate mechanisms of our elaborate technology or social organization. Our society simply must, for its own safety and for the welfare of its citizens, find and train this kind of talent for abstract thinking, for the intricate juggling of the mind wrestling with complex interrelationships among men and matter.

State universities have peculiar opportunities to play a role here. Since there are different levels of intellectual talent, and differential rates of development in its use, it is only good sense to recognize these in the instructional situation. I admit, however, that there are some serious and difficult issues here. Since students are inevitably taught in groups, should they be grouped in ability levels? Dael Wolfle in his study, *America's Resources of Specialized Talent,* has described the great variations which actually exist in the student populations of different colleges. Some are so selective that almost all their graduates rate on an intelligence scale above the average of all college graduates, while others are so selective in reverse, so to speak, that almost all their graduates fall below the average in intelligence of all college graduates. In view of these differences among colleges, Bruno Fricke, in a challenging article on admissions policies, has suggested that it would be reasonable for each college to determine the normal ability level of its students, and then to decline admission to those applicants who fall below the established range of ability. With this proposal there would be some, but not so much, argument. But then he goes on to suggest that it would be equally reasonable to decline admission to a student whose ability is above the established range, on the grounds that he would be better served by finding a college whose student population more nearly approximated his own level of ability. This proposal is guaranteed to be provocative. Is it valid? It is at least a good bone of contention for discussion in academic circles.

How homogeneous in ability levels should a college population be? And what kind of an undergraduate population should a state university have? For the sake of argument, I am willing to propose that the undergraduate students admitted to the peculiar environment of the state university should give evidence of superior intellectual ability; should have demonstrated academic achievement of a high order; should reveal sufficient curiosity to suggest that they can profit from the tutelage of a faculty, a large part of which is engaged in scholarly research or creative contribution to professions; and should indicate a desire for at least four years of college, with the possible capacity for continuing beyond this for graduate or professional training. Having gone this far, I would also suggest that the faculty should be prepared to recognize differences even within this group by providing honors courses throughout the four years as additional stimulation for the very brightest students. Let me hasten to add that the development of this much flexibility in the undergraduate program costs money and would bring the cost of undergraduate education closer to the level of cost of graduate education. The level of financial support currently received by most of our universities is still too low to permit as much improvement in instruction as would be desirable, not only for the very brightest students, but even for all who are admitted.

In suggesting the desirability of this much selectivity at the state university, I am *not* suggesting that *only* the very highest levels of intellectual ability should be recognized in our society and given educational opportunities beyond the high school. If we could only be honest enough to admit that in terms of intellectual ability (I am not talking about virtue or usefulness) there are differences, we could then assert with pride that in the United States we have tried through our educational institutions to develop not only the Grade A and B intellectual levels but also the Grade C. Our very brightest products can be surrounded and assisted in what only they can achieve by very useful and very admirable helpers. In most of our states the long-established state university has peculiar resources and peculiar opportunities for students of superior intellectual ability, and should by all means be enabled to serve them well. Other institutions in the state can and should be supported to serve those individuals headed for many kinds of useful and honorable careers who may not possess the abilities for more arduous intellectual labor which can be stimulated and disciplined by the more strenuous environment of the state university.

Here, then, is an issue. Does such segregation according to ability levels automatically imply snobbishness? Does it encourage a dangerous tendency toward the creation of an aristocratic elite? It already exists to a degree among college populations. Should this fact be recognized and accepted, or resisted? What effect should it have on planning for the state university and other institutions in the state?

Here, then, is a set of issues affecting undergraduate education in our state universities. How should the role of the faculty man within the state university be defined so as to permit him to fulfill the obligations he incurs? What kind of a personnel policy is required? How should faculties be organized for the handling of their affairs in relation to their responsibilities, among others, to undergraduates? How should the faculties be interrelated so as to care for their service-course obligations? How far should faculties go in helping beginning undergraduates find their way, amid all the varied alternatives appropriate to the state university, toward the opportunities most suited to their own interests and potentialities? What kinds of students should be admitted to the state university? What should the state university do about special programming for the very brightest students?

In presenting this list of questions as issues confronting undergraduate education in the state university, I have aired some of my own choices and some of my own prejudices with a view to provoking discussion and thought. I am well aware that each and every educator has his own choices in the matter, and I am sure that the area of undergraduate education will be given the serious consideration it deserves.

Graduate Education and Research

By Sanford S. Atwood

Of the many challenges which a university faces, one of the most important, if not *the* most important, involves its program of graduate education and research. Since a university, by definition, must include graduate education and research in a wide variety of fields, our attention should be focused primarily on the degree of distinction in this area. It is my contention that to be a *great* university today, and probably for the foreseeable future, it is absolutely essential that the university should strive continually for a position of pre-eminence in graduate education and research.

Since such a challenge applies to every institution of note the question arises as to what degree of pre-eminence is obtainable. Since not all of us can be in the first ranks, how much prestige is practical? Among the deans of the 41 institutions represented in the Association of Graduate Schools, one finds general agreement that all in the group consider themselves to be prestige institutions. And this might be conceded if we recall that among the more than 1800 institutions of higher education in the United States, only 266 of them have conferred the doctorate as an earned degree, and only 165 granted such degrees last year.

But when issues are clearly drawn, as for example on the allocation of Woodrow Wilson Fellows, then it becomes apparent that there are superprestige institutions among the prestige institutions. Of the 700 applicants who were selected by the Woodrow Wilson regional boards last year, 25 per cent of them designated Harvard as their number one preference. All of us know the factors which have conditioned this phenomenon, and we know the practical remedies that are being developed, but it is clear that in at least the collective mind of this particular public, there is a real degree of distinction now conferred upon Harvard that all of us might seek to emulate.

The figures on total degrees awarded enforce this assertion. The first Ph.D. degrees in this country were awarded to three men by Yale University in 1861. Since then, each of the 10 leading institutions has granted more than 4,000 degrees; each of the next 19 institutions has conferred over 1,000 degrees; and each of the next 25 institutions has conferred over 500 degrees. Expressing this in percentages of the grand total of over 131,000 degrees conferred through 1955, the first 10 institutions have been responsible for 44 per cent of the total, the first 29 institutions for 75 per cent, and the first 54 for 90 per cent.

In passing, it might be noted that privately controlled institutions have accounted for the major share of this production. Among the first 10, 6 are privately controlled, and they granted approximately two thirds of all degrees in that group. Among the first 29, 16 are private, and they awarded about 60 per cent of the total in the group.

Clearly, prestige in graduate education is a relative matter. There are no clear-cut levels of distinction. In effect, with the diversity of patterns now prevalent among different schools, each of us competes with the schools immediately above or below us in the peck-order, and each of us tries to improve our Chicago *Tribune* rating. This situation even varies from field to field within an institution. I find that some of my

Cornell colleagues, particularly those in the humanities, measure their prestige against a background of ivy colleges. Others turn westward and are more concerned with the burgeoning size and significance of the great land-grant colleges and state universities.

Size of operation is, of course, only one standard of measure. As the race intensifies, and as the publicly supported schools inevitably assume a greater share of the load, quality will be a measure of increasing importance. Let's face it, the prestige of graduate education is a factor to be reckoned with continually by every institution, and over-all pre-eminence of both quantity and quality should be an essential goal.

The importance of graduate education in the United States today is emphasized by the statistics on its constantly increasing volume. In general, the number of doctorates has essentially doubled in each decade since they were first granted. This is approximately equivalent to an increment of 7 per cent per annum. In that first decade of the 1860's, only 16 degrees were awarded, but by the first decade of this century the total was 3,654. In the 1930's, the number was 27,468, and it is estimated that the 1950's will produce nearly 75,000. In other words, of all doctoral degrees conferred in the last 100 years, approximately half have been granted in the last 10 years.

This leads to one of my generalizations, namely that graduate education and research are more vital to our way of life today than they ever have been, and their relative importance in the over-all educational process is constantly increasing with no leveling in sight. This assertion, I believe, can be verified independently for graduate education and for research. It follows, then, that each state should do all in its power to promote at least one principal center for graduate education in the broadest sense. This institution should have faculties in all important fields of knowledge, but it might well emphasize those that are peculiar to the geography or resources of the state. It should attract all possible financial support to build its libraries, laboratories, and physical facilities so that outstanding teachers and students are attracted, thereby resulting in the kind of trained scholars who can carry out the obligations of the future.

Graduate education is the principal supplier of highly trained persons in a wide variety of fields, professional and nonprofessional alike, but it is most important as the mechanism for training each successive generation of teachers, or at least the teachers of the teachers. It is like sorting out the best seed to grow the next crop. This is the kind of responsibility that would seem to demand the most careful planning, but in general the process has not been as orderly, or as well organized, as some would like to see it. At least in comparison with the medical profession, for example, where the number of doctors is closely integrated with over-all needs, in college and university teaching we seem to replace planning with chance. By 1970 we are faced with a need for doubling the number of college teachers, as well as for upgrading through better-trained replacements, and all that we seem to be doing is to let the system roll along with the hope that the next decade will somehow produce a doubling as has each decade in the past. Granted that we might assume this much faith in the system, even casual survey shows that the supply will certainly lag in relation to the demand and that the relative needs of various fields are haphazardly predicted at best.

A similar situation confronts us in the training of capable research workers. Apparently, the more we supply, the greater is the demand. Our way of life in this country has become geared to a constant outpouring of new ideas, not only for the further growth of our standard of living, but even as a prime force in holding our economic levels from slipping backward.

From this, I certainly don't mean to infer that social planners need take over the operation of our graduate schools. No, if the system is operating well, it will provide the needed flexibility. Let me give a couple of examples of what I mean by flexibility. To be sure, a man with a Ph.D. in bacteriology is a highly specialized creature, but if his training is sufficiently broad, he should be capable of either teaching or conducting research in a range of related fields such as botany, plant pathology, biochemistry or genetics. Or with the history major whose thesis is an intensive study of one man in a limited period, a shift to other types of research or to broad-scale teaching of the history of any period should be easy if his Ph.D. is of the quality we are trying to produce by emphasizing attitudes and methods rather than specific subject matter.

It is granted that with a market demand for both college teachers and research personnel far exceeding the prospective supply, and with low teaching salaries making the opportunities there relatively unattractive, we may be tempted to control our output more rigorously and to classify our products more specifically for certain jobs. This, I maintain, would be self-defeating and would lead to the same degeneration of our highest earned degree that has already taken place in the high school. No, let's keep a flexible system that trains the maximum capacities of each individual and that allows each institution to use its particular resources for the maximum number and quality of trainees that it can afford.

The problem, even with flexibility of both opportunity and training, is to match up each new student with the professor who is best suited to be his mentor. This combination should be compatible from the personal aspects, but it also must be sufficiently stimulating from the intellectual aspects to maximize the student's capabilities. Granted that an undergraduate has usually settled on his major field of interest in only general terms, how are we to guide him to the graduate opportunities that will be best for him?

There is a temptation to advise him mainly on the relative merits of different schools, but I would like to promote the concept of matching the student with a particular professor. To be sure, part of the particular professor's effectiveness will depend on the kind of environment in which he is teaching. Does he have the necessary resources of libraries and laboratories? Does he have colleagues who will provide the proper breadth of training? Are there other students who cumulatively provide the right atmosphere for work and stimulation? All of these and other characteristics are important in the choice, but of greatest importance is the man with whom the student will study.

This ideal matching is far from easy, and considering all of the human vagaries that are involved, it's a wonder that we make ideal, or even near-ideal, connections as often as we do. My reason, however, for emphasizing the desirability of striving to perfect these student-teacher relationships is not only for the sake of the students and of the teachers themselves, but mainly because I believe a concerted national effort in this direction would do a great deal to utilize many of our resources in graduate education that are not now being utilized to capacity.

Too often when we take a quick look at graduate education in this country, we are tempted to pay special attention to the top five, or maybe the leading twenty-five, graduate schools. We may even equate quality with quantity, and the result seems only to make the best ones better. We need more than this, however, if we want to reach a doubling of the Ph.D. output in the next decade. We need to utilize every teacher, not just those in the large departments in the large institutions. By utilizing every teacher, wherever he may be and in whatever school he is located —yes, every good teacher who can duplicate his kind through graduate training—and by turning this into a mass effort, the needed greater numbers can be achieved, and every participating school will thereby be automatically raising its prestige rating.

In this period of dynamic change in graduate education and research, it is natural that certain critics should be sniping at any weakness observable in the system. Often these criticisms are spoken by outsiders, who quite properly resent the snobbishness that sometimes accompanies a high level of training. It may even take the form of anti-intellectualism, and here we should fight back on the grounds that part of democracy's function is to maximize individual ability. Special instruction for the gifted is an inherent principle in graduate education, and the system should be flexible enough to allow the best possible training in creative scholarship for each individual.

This pastime of criticizing graduate education has extended, however, to some of the graduate deans, and thereby deserves more serious notice. In a report submitted last year by a committee of four deans of the Association of Graduate Schools, this statement is made:

We must ruefully conclude that the Ph.D. is tortuously slow and riddled with needless uncertainties; that it is frequently inefficient and traumatically disagreeable to the bewildered and frustrated candidate. The basic flaw is: we have never cleanly defined this protean degree.

On the graduate deans' rueful attitude, I must agree if we examine only the statistics for certain graduate schools, especially those in large metropolitan areas with a high proportion of part-time students. But their concern is not applicable if we focus on some of the leading graduate schools where a high proportion of the students are Ph.D. candidates engaged straight through on full-time programs supported by fellowships and assistantships.

With part-time study the process is slow, and the deans rightfully commented that "generally the Ph.D. takes at least four years to get; more often it takes six or seven, and not infrequently ten to fifteen." If this is so, then these deans should change their system. Other schools have shown that this slow progress is not a necessary part of graduate education.

The deans' suggestion about the time for a Ph.D. is that "the whole program should take no more than three years of residence." This to me is a violation of a basic principle that has kept the Ph.D. respectable when most other degrees have deteriorated. It is quite proper to have a *minimum* residence requirement of three years, but a maximum, no! Under the present system of a minimum but not a maximum residence requirement, any of us can say to the *few outstanding* students that the minimum requirement may be all that will be required for earning their degrees. The remaining students will be distributed in some kind of a normal curve. The average student will take longer to reach the same level of accomplishment, and a few may eventually reach the mark by persistent and forced work over a still longer period. The only problem here for graduate faculties is to be strict enough not only at admission but at every step in the process so that a proper standard for granting the degree is maintained. I am not proposing that we select only Methuselahs for graduate study or that we encourage undue extension of the programs, since some reasonable limit of five to seven years may be in order, but let's not have a maximum that sets unreal standards or fails to recognize individual differences. If we should adopt a maximum period of residence, then it would follow that we should award the degree with accompanying grades or levels of distinction. In my opinion, the present system is preferable, if we can agree both within and between institutions to the maintenance of adequate minimum standards of scholarship.

The deans' comment about uncertainties leaves me cold. This might apply to high school work, or even undergraduate and professional training. In contrast, the Ph.D. must be riddled with uncertainties if the objective is to explore the unknown and to produce original research and scholarly effort. Some schools may have extended the uncertainties needlessly to various administrative mechanisms for recording progress toward the goal, and if so, let them get rid of such factors, but let's not try to remove the uncertainty from research. If we do, it will no longer be research in the true sense.

In regard to the deans' final inference that we might reduce the traumas and frustrations if we *cleanly* defined the degree, I would suggest that this has been done for many years by thinking faculties. The record is clear, but I will cite only from my own institution since it is the case with which I am most familiar.

Our Code of Legislation states the Purpose and Nature of Graduate Study in these simple terms:

It is the purpose of the Graduate School to offer facilities for advanced study and research so that students may obtain a comprehensive view of a field of knowledge and receive the training required for independent investigation in that field.

That's all there is to it. That's all it takes to define "cleanly" the work for a degree.

The paragraph continues:

In providing this opportunity, the School makes it possible for the students to associate freely with mature scholars who will give them such aid and direction as they may need. Accomplishment is judged primarily by the evidence of the growing capacity for critical thought and mastery of the subject matter in a selected field of study and not by the fulfillment of routine requirements.

To me, this is a *clean* definition. And it operates without being disagreeable to frustrated candidates. To be sure, it needs a faculty dedicated to operating it fairly and expeditiously. It means, however, that the requirements for an advanced degree are very simple:

1. a period of study in residence
2. the mastery of certain subjects as measured by examinations, and
3. the presentation of a satisfactory thesis.

Yes, it is possible for a candidate to complete a degree at Cornell without a single course or credit appearing on his transcript. I'll admit that this would be the unusual case, since most students find it efficient use of their own and faculty time to enroll in some graduate courses or seminars. But the only requirements that must be completed are the residence, the exams, and the thesis.

Rather than change the residence requirement from a minimum to a maximum time, I would prefer seeing the residence aspect abolished altogether. Then a degree would be awarded on the judgment of the faculty when the man has displayed sufficient capacity as shown only by his examinations and his thesis. To this might be added the criterion used by Welsh universities that the degree is awarded only after continued productiveness in research is demonstrated over a period of years.

It is my strong conviction that when graduate work is defined in greater detail and when part-time programs are encouraged, the deans themselves will become bewildered and will send up a cry for help. Some of you may think that I am oversimplifying the process because you have seen our Code of Legislation running to more than twenty-five finely printed pages. This, I maintain, is simply good housekeeping, making it easier for the students and staff alike to know what is required and how to meet the general requirements, all with a minimum of administrative overhead. I do not believe that it is possible to legislate any more detailed standards than the general requirements. This is a responsibility that must be borne first by the students, and second by the professors individually for their own students and to a certain degree collectively within fields. In essence, graduate education is an apprentice relationship. The student learns how to do research—how to think analytically and originally—by doing it. There is no other way than by doing it. Under the guidance of his mentors, he establishes both the substance and the quality of his scholarship. He learns not only methods, skills, techniques, facts, and experience, but also moral standards, judgment, and breadth of viewpoint—in short, he aims at the Ph.D. degree "which sets out to nurture individual discovery and which exalts newness in knowledge." In practice this apprenticeship may be carried one step further through postdoctoral fellowships, which can be equated to the internship and residence of the medical profession. Those of us hiring new staff members recognize the value of this continued apprentice experience for the persons outstandingly qualified. It is generally noted that this type of experience is probably the best guarantee of a man's genuine interest and ability in research and of such interest and productiveness continuing throughout his career.

My rebuttal to the graduate deans is intended to help remove some of the myth that they claim has enveloped the Ph.D. It is my contention that most of the myth has been unduly conjured up by the deans themselves. It is certainly not present in the hard day-to-day market place where Ph.D. degrees are receiving proper recognition by all kinds of employers, including colleges, government, and industry. Even the students know the value, so it remains for the professors to see that each degree awarded is worthy of the title.

Some other general ideas prevail in our concepts of graduate education and research, and I would like to comment on them likewise.

For example, why do we constantly debate the relative value of basic and applied research? Both are essential, and in any well-ordered system of research effort, an equilibrium is reached between them. Ideally, at least in the setting of a state university, each staff member should have interest and capabilities in both types. In actuality, the line between basic and applied is not clear-cut, and there is a complete range of problems extending from entirely fundamental to wholly practical. But each gives impetus to the other, and the well-trained research worker should be able to shift his emphasis as the needs of the particular investigation demand. Recently, when Dr. Von Braun was questioned on his definition of basic research, he said that it is "when I am doing what I don't know what I'm doing." For a somewhat fuller definition that seems to cover all research, I like the version supplied by Dr. J. H. Means:

In its essence research may be said to be man's conscious effort to find new facts by exploration, to relate them one to another, and to derive from them new principles and generalizations. It is the consequence of man's insatiable curiosity and of his innate desire to improve his own lot. In the long-range view, progress through research discloses itself as an evolutionary process. We may draw an analogy between the research performed consciously and with intent by man and unconscious research on the part of nature. As man sets up experiments to find new truth, so does nature, in the case of living organisms at least, make experimental types through the process of mutation and test them out in the struggle for existence. Thus we believe has the evolution of species come about, and in similar fashion so has man acquired new knowledge and learned to improve his ways of approaching his objectives. As does nature, under an irresistible drive to procreate, force life to adapt itself to every environment, no matter how inimical, capable of supporting life at all, so does man, under his drive to know, inquire into and explore every region of his cosmos to which his sensibilities and his intelligence direct him.

If you accept this broad definition of research, it seems useless to debate the merits of basic vs. applied research. Why not, instead, grant that a university which covers the gamut from basic to applied will provide the best atmosphere for the broad-scale graduate training and research effort that is needed in every state?

This leads to an important corollary idea, namely, whether or not we are providing training that will let the next generation keep up adequately with advancing knowledge. Dr. Oppenheimer has suggested that whereas only a few years ago the sum total of man's knowledge was doubling each fifty years, today the process is accelerated to the point of doubling each ten years. Dean De Vane in a recent book asked if we are really reaching the limit of the mind. Considering the increments in knowledge at the current rate, is it possible for one mind to encompass and collate all of the new ideas? Does this fact help to explain our widely heralded drift to conformity? Is the break-through going to come from machines with greater capacity than any one mind, providing thereby an intellectual revolution comparable to the industrial revolution?

By posing these questions, I don't mean to imply that we should base all of our hopes on some new, simplified, and more efficient method of learning. No, as a biologist I must concur with Professor Petry when he said, "Unless the history of man's development is a wholly false guide, the improvement of educational method by some revolutionary break-through of technique is as improbable as the sudden development of some new method of human reproduction."

In answering these questions, we might focus on the aspects related to our present methods of graduate training. It can be predicted that at least some of the present crop of graduate students will continue in their research careers until the year 2000. Shouldn't we ask ourselves whether our training is in broad enough fundamentals, or at least with sufficient motivation for continued self-improvement, to prepare for careers extending to the end of this millennium? Let's be sure that we are not giving our graduate students only the simple problems that we understand and would do ourselves if we had the time. Let's be sure that every thesis is not only publishable but also published.

My remarks here and at other places in this paper sound remarkably similar to many of those in the Report of Panel V, sponsored by the Rockefeller Brothers Fund. I can assure you, however, that my manuscript was composed before this Report was available to me. It is most comforting, therefore, to find the Report likewise emphasizing the need for preparing ourselves "for a constant and growing demand for talents of all varieties." Apparently we are in perfect agreement on the urgency of educating "our young people to meet an unknown need rather than to prepare them for needs already identified."

It follows also that we should be doing everything possible to attract the very best brains into graduate study, as well as to develop each one to its maximum capacity. As a nation we have expressed great concern about the attrition of well-qualified students between high school and college. But I propose that there is an even more important loss between the bachelor's and doctor's degrees. To arrive at valid figures that would prove the point is most difficult because we are not sure of the character we're measuring. It is even difficult to verbalize the distinction. Let me put the distinction between undergraduate and graduate work in the words of one of our professors of electrical engineering:

The principal function of undergraduate education should be to develop the mind of a student by having him think through things that other people have frequently thought through before. It should be the object of undergraduate education to pursue this process to the point where it is no longer worth the student's while to think through well-known thoughts merely in order to develop his mind. Graduation should signify that the student's mind is about as developed as it can be merely by studying what is well known. By contrast, it should be the object of graduate education to develop the student's mind by having him think through things that have not been completely thought through before so far as the student is aware. Research should thus be the principal tool of graduate education.

Professor Booker did *not* say that our acquisition of factual knowledge is completed with the baccalaureate. No, he simply said that every student reaches a point of diminishing returns with regard to the process of rethinking concepts that are already known. Hopefully, each student will continue to accumulate more and better facts and attitudes—a liberal education, if you will—throughout the rest of his life in the best tradition of adult education. But when he begins graduate work, he engages in a new process, namely, "to think through things that have not been completely thought through before."

To select for this basic characteristic of graduate education—the ability to think through thoughts that nobody has thought through before —we need better measures than are now available. Wouldn't we agree also that too much of the educational process that now leads up to a bachelor's degree is based on fixed curricula and routine learning that tend to stifle originality and imagination? It is a wonder to me that we get as many good brains as we do to enter this higher phase where originality and imagination have premium value. Recall the rigor of selection that is involved. For every thirty-nine first-level degrees awarded last year, there was only one doctorate.

For a continued advance of scientific research and scholarship, we should depend less on chance selection of students. We need first to foster the qualities necessary for graduate work throughout the undergraduate years, and even in high school, and then to provide better opportunities to develop every good research brain that now may be lost in the shuffle. As was pointed out forcefully in the Stanford study, "all scholars and graduate students are undergraduates first." Let us preserve in the undergraduate curriculum those aspects that will identify, stimulate, segregate, and prepare the potential graduate student.

One more provocation. Granted that our methods of graduate education might be improved, why shouldn't we attempt to refine the definition of the Ph.D. by strengthening the aspect for which it has always been intended, namely the highest level of research and scholarship, and then dignifying each alternative professional degree for its proper place in the over-all scheme. Through 1916, over 96 per cent of all doctorates were the Ph.D. The others were Doctor of Science (1.4 per cent), Doctor of Pedagogy (1.3 per cent), and doctorates in civil law, sacred theology, literature, public health, music, and engineering. In recent years, the Doctor of Education has become the second most frequent doctorate. Other professional or nonresearch degrees (such as M.D., D.D.S., D.V.M., or J.S.D.), may carry the title of doctor but they are not the equivalent of the Ph.D. in qualitative requirements. They may represent the same length of time in study, and they may aim for the same general level of attainment, but they are distinctly professional in character and do not embody the broad research aims of the Ph.D.

Whenever this subject is discussed, one encounters individuals who are concerned over the problems that must be faced in setting a new pattern. This does not bother me, however, because I have every confidence that the new patterns will soon reach equilibrium in the free market once the standards are clearly understood. Again I must cite Cornell examples for they are the ones with which I am most familiar. Cornell was the first school to establish a five-year pattern for architecture. It was pioneering at the time, but now all accredited schools of architecture have five-year programs. Cornell led the way in a five-year program to a bachelor's degree in engineering. Even though relatively few engineering colleges have adopted the five-year bachelor's curriculum, this has not raised any problems about our selling a premium product; quite the contrary has been the case. Likewise, when we established a graduate program in business and public administration, it was based on two years of post-baccalaureate work and led to the master's degree. This degree, which is significantly different from others of its general kind, has now reached equilibrium in the market, and its holders are remunerated accordingly. Similarly, we expect professional doctorates to assume their rightful place. I'm not asking for a needless proliferation of degrees. Rather the job ahead seems to be one of giving proper emphasis to each professional doctor's degree and operating it with clearly defined standards that separate it from the Ph.D. with something more than a differential in the language requirement.

I would like to close with one general assertion about the future. Here my point can best be made by an analogy with my own professional interests as a geneticist and plant breeder. When the breeder is confronted with a situation in which the mutation frequency is high, providing thereby a wide range of variability, he knows that improvement is possible. He can be confident that if he applies adequate selection pressures, the desired objectives will be obtained. Similarly, in graduate education and research today, we are dealing with a situation where the rate of change is high and where the whole system is dynamic, at least in comparison with the more static European system. In the United States, I believe, we can count on a public demand to maintain the selection pressure at a level where the changes that will occur in the next twenty-five years will seem explosive. With sufficient effort devoted to making graduate education and research a vital and increasingly important part of the University's endeavor, we can guarantee that by the time the University of Texas celebrates its centennial, the changes that have occurred in these first seventy-five years will seem small in comparison.

The University and Public Service

By O. Meredith Wilson

Few assigned topics have given me so much trouble as has this one. My first difficulties have been with definition. What is intended by "public service"? There is, of course, an imposing bibliography, of which Joseph E. McLean's *The Public Service and University Education* is a fitting example; and there is an academic community concerned with that bibliography; and there is a practicing quasi-professional corps, all of which would suggest that my discussion should be focused on the developing schools of public administration and the emerging professional bureaucracy which they train. Thomas Jefferson proposed a professorship of Law and Police at William and Mary College as a possible approach to the problem. David E. Lilienthal, in a commencement address given over 150 years later at the University of Virginia, recommended that we educate a public qualified and interested enough to phase in and out of government service—that is, prepared to devote one large block of their lives to government in order to make unnecessary the development of a class of separated professional bureaucrats. In the intervening years the problem has enlisted the speculation of our best and most interested citizens. Somewhere in the murky waters of modern public policy, perhaps jostled by Milovan Djilas' *The New Class* on the one hand, and C. Northcote Parkinson's scientific formulae on the other, an American answer to this particular problem of public service may be found. Properly undertaken, an effort at finding the answer would be appropriate at these festivities; so also, a colonel's tunic would be an appropriate costume at a formal dinner, but you'd hardly expect Brigitte Bardot to be the one to wear it. I have, therefore, looked further for my theme.

There is also a rather formalized term "public service," that can be discovered in most faculty evaluation systems. On the dosier of most staff members there is likely to appear a list of his good works; for example, "spoke at high school for Rotary Career Day; served as captain of United Fund, 'Academic Section'; appointed a member of the city planning commission;" etc. Here, perhaps, I have competence, but the topic is unworthy.

There seemed left to me one alternative—to open a discussion on the question: In what way can a university be of the greatest possible public service? With months to correspond, I might have asked the Texas Committee to clarify their intent in posing the issue of public service. My reason for not doing so is clear. It is a dangerous thing for one person to ask of another too specifically what he should say. It can lead to surprising difficulties, as is illustrated in the experience of the young boy who asked his father what to say in a short biography of King Alfred the Great. The father gave his son a bibliography and a warning: "Mind you, son, the story of Alfred, the woman, and the burnt cakes has been told so often that I wouldn't repeat it if I were you." When the son's story was read to his class it was excellent until he came to the last line which read, "and then of course Alfred went to visit a certain lady, but the less said about that the better." The choice of direction in the following remarks has been my own.

There is real difficulty in reaching a definition of a university, but the problem is simplified by the nature of the festival. We are discussing the genius of a university, and, in its embodiment, the University of Texas. There are special overtones of character and history that are determined by the fact that Texas is a public, a state, university. The following quotation from Thorstein Veblen about the state university may provide the perspective from which to begin the discussion: How can a university be of the greatest possible public service? In *Higher Learning in America*, Veblen says, speaking of the American university as a class:

Although the illustration is by no means uniformly convincing [the] greater number of these state schools are not, or are not yet, universities except in name. These establishments have been founded, commonly, with a professed utilitarian purpose, and have started out with professional training as their chief avowed aim. The purpose made most of in their establishment has commonly been to train young men for proficiency in some gainful occupation; along with this have gone many half-articulate professions of solicitude for cultural interests to be taken care of by the same means. They have been installed by politicians looking for popular acclaim, rather than by men of scholarly or scientific insight, and their management has not infrequently been entrusted to political masters of intrigue, with scant academic qualifications; their foundation has been the work of practical politicians with a view to conciliate the good will of a lay constituency clamouring for things tangibly "useful"—that is to say, pecuniarily gainful. So these experts in short-term political prestige have made provision for schools of a "practical" character; but they have named these establishments "universities" because the name carries an air of scholarly repute, of a higher, more substantial kind than any naked avowal of material practicality would give. Yet, in those instances where the passage of time has allowed the readjustment to take place, these quasi- "universities," installed by men of affairs, of a crass "practicality," and in response to the utilitarian demands of an unlearned political constituency, have in the long run taken on more and more of an academic, non-utilitarian character, and have been gradually falling into line as universities claiming a place among the seminaries of the higher learning. The long-term drift of modern cultural ideals leaves these schools no final resting place short of the university type, however far short of such a consummation the greater number of them may still be found.

There is a truth that lurks in the irony of Veblen. There are, of course, public educational institutions that were the children of politics, and that have been used as political pawns. But the American state university is a legitimate child of American culture and not simply a handy device for political exploitation. The American people are addicted to a form of cultural optimism which Alexis de Tocqueville described as a belief in the indefinite perfectibility of man. In the grip of this optimistic faith the American not only expects but demands progress. For him today is not lived for today but as preparation for tomorrow. As one bicultural member of our community (half Sioux, half German) expressed it while trying to illustrate the difference between the time-conscious European-American and the time-indifferent Sioux, his brethren: "the American looks at his watch, not to learn what time it is, but to see what time it isn't quite yet." That, characteristically, we are always preparing for a time that isn't quite yet was confirmed to Tocqueville in the most surprising places. In *Democracy in America* he mentions an instance:

I accost an American sailor and inquire why the ships of his country are built so as to last for only a short time; he answers without hesitation that the art of navigation is everyday making such rapid progress that the finest vessel would become almost useless if it lasted beyond a few years.

In the grip of this optimism we have considered it necessary to prepare for progress. The one most consciously developed instrument for ministering to the needs of progress has been institutionalized education. Thomas Jefferson saw public education as the machinery required for progress in self-government; Horace Mann as the means to genuine equality; and Whitehead, in the conditions of modern life, as the means of survival. In a frontier society consciously inventing a social instrument to minister to the demands of progress, it would be unnatural to expect a "temple of pure knowledge." There need be nothing invidious in an observation that the state university was "founded, commonly, with a profound utilitarian purpose," or "to train young men for proficiency in some gainful occupation." There was a world of undefeated land, natural resources lay around in rich profusion, the raw materials required for material comforts abounded, but comfort itself was rare. If education were to be enlisted in the battle against nature, the expectation of the frontier American must have been that applied science could improve the estate of man. Europe could be depended upon for reflection, meditation, curiosity, knowledge for its own sake; from American science, more immediate and practical results must be asked. Nor is this practical orientation surprising in a democratic society; for in such a society impatience with excessive theory, and suspicion of anyone who admits to being superior in any way, are matched by the assumption that all things shall be judged by their contribution to the peace, comfort, and prosperity of the individual members. Therefore, the entry of public money, under democratic aegis, into the field of post–high school education was quite naturally responsible for agricultural and mechanical colleges, or for universities that emphasized business and the professions, and were willing to bend their efforts toward solving immediate and practical, i.e., pecuniary, problems.

An examination of its origins reveals that the tradition of the state university is the tradition of public service. If engineers are needed, there a school of engineering shall be established; so, too, with doctor, lawyer, merchant, and chief. Look at the bulletin of any large state university. You will find in its list of schools a catalogue of the modern professions. These schools were established as a response to social need and in the tradition that the university is a consciously designed instrument by which society promotes progress. It is not necessary to counsel institutions sponsored by a democratic society to support the practical sciences, nor to ask them to prepare for the public services a body of trained men, nor to apply their tools of knowledge toward immediate social gains. The organized farmer presses for agricultural progress. The cities insist upon municipal research and planning. The bar and the medical society make their demands and constantly query the results of formal education, using the practical norms of the courtroom and bedside to criticize the theoreticians of the classroom. Road building, architecture, pharmacy, veterinary medicine, hotel management, accounting, all are courses reflecting public need and public demand in the academic mirror. That American universities were founded to perform specific services for particular publics is confirmed by a letter from Thomas Jefferson to Peter Carr, dated September 7, 1814. Because he could not attend a meeting of a Board of Trustees which was to become the Board of the University of Virginia, Jefferson wrote his impressions for Carr's use. Having examined seminaries in other countries, he says:

I am struck with the diversity of arrangement observable in them—no two alike. . . . The example they set . . . is authority for us to select from their different institutions the materials which are good for us, and, with them, to erect a structure, whose arrangement shall correspond with our own social condition.

After thus rooting the academic structure firmly in its proper sociological garden, he proceeded to recommend a series of academic functions not only to benefit the usual professions but also, through an inchoate extension division, to serve the "mariner, carpenter, shipwright, pumpmaker, clockmaker, machinist, optician, metallurgist, founder, cutler, druggist, brewer, vintner, distiller, dyer, painter, bleacher, soapmaker, tanner, powdermaker, saltmaker, glassmaker, to learn as much as shall be necessary to pursue their art understandingly. . . ."

There can be no question that public service—that is, education for immediate practical consequences—was a prime consideration for Jefferson as he contemplated the development of one university. We should, therefore, feel no embarrassment as we explore the road to the highest public service for the state university of today.

The high road to service is hinted at in Veblen's remarks quoted earlier. Born of the utilitarian demands of an unlearned political constituency, the state institution began as a practical servant of progress; experience has demonstrated that the ultimate utility is theoretical knowledge; so these institutions of applied knowledge have been pulled inexorably toward true university characterisics; "the long-term drift of modern cultural ideals leaves these schools no final resting place short of the university type." But this is more than a drift. It is the description of a healthy social institution growing in the direction that its task requires.

That this was the direction in which the highest public service lay was recognized by Tocqueville a hundred and twenty-five years ago:

I am convinced, that if the Americans had been alone in the world, with the freedom and the knowledge acquired by their forefathers and the passions which are their own, they would not have been slow to discover that progress cannot long be made in the application of the sciences without cultivating the theory of them; that all the arts are perfected by one another; and, however absorbed they might have been by the pursuit of the principal object of their desires, they would speedily have admitted that it is necessary to turn aside from it occasionally in order the better to attain it in the end.

... possessing education and freedom, men living in democratic ages cannot fail to improve the industrial part of science. . . . Henceforward all the efforts of the constituted authorities ought to be directed to support the highest branches of learning and to foster the nobler passion for science itself. In the present age the human mind needs to be coerced into theoretical studies; it runs of its own accord to practical applications.

Acceptance of Tocqueville's diagnosis of the importance of meditation to science and of the characteristic shortcomings of democracy underlines the need of our being consciously alerted to the importance of fostering the passion for science itself. Tocqueville says:

Nothing is more necessary to the culture of the higher sciences or of the elevated departments of science than meditation; and nothing is less suited to meditation than the structure of democratic society.

Tocqueville, in searching for the pulse of democratic America, only incidentally dealt with the mission of education and the effect of democratic society upon it. Many men since have more self-consciously attacked the problem. Ortega y Gassett, in his effort to define the mission, that is, the proper public service, of a university was led to treat the university as an analogue of the medieval city. But to be sure of myself I should like to use his symbolism in my own way. The medieval city began as a walled fortress at the crossing place of a large river, or at a strategic point on the path of trade. Merchants passing by pitched their camp under the protecting shadow of the burg, paid a tribute or fee for the privilege, hawked some goods at the local fair. Gradually there developed under the protecting influence of the city and its garrison *faubourgs*, outside the walls, that provided trade and commerce and enriched the city itself. But the tradesmen outside the walls were dependent. Their own security was drawn from the central city. If it were to decay, the merchants would be forced to flee to another haven, or failing this to wither in wealth and activity. The *faubourgs* were capable of enriching and adorning the life of the city; they were ultimately to engulf it; but originally they were defenseless petitioners for protection, not fundamental elements of its strength.

The central city in a university is that part which interprets and transmits the vital system of ideas which we describe as the culture of the race; it is that part which engages in the role of criticism, judgment, and evaluation of the existing institutions, which encourages and supports the meditation and speculative process—by which existing premises are questioned, new hypotheses adumbrated and tested, and by which we continue to satisfy man's curiosity about fundamental or pure knowledge. For convenience, though it means various things to various people, I will call it the college of science and the humanities. As advances were made in science some men became interested in the application of theories of thermodynamics to the development of motive power. They were translating pure knowledge into public service. In the process, engineering schools were established as *faubourgs* under the walls of the central city. Others interpreted and translated anatomical, botanical, chemical, and physical theories in the interest of human health. Some of these medical men were late in coming from the hospital and the physicians' office to the university, but since the early days of the University of Salerno the medical school has synthesized and applied pure science to human health. It is significant to my argument to note how Flexner's report triggered a quick change from instruction by practicing physicians to instruction by full-time academic physicians who now seek the closest possible relation between the university and medicine. The chief concern now is that the medical arts should draw as close as possible to the engines of research, so that no lag can develop between medical practice and the developing science upon which good medicine must depend.

In like manner, but in later season, business schools developed to apply the knowledge made available by economists, psychologists, and sociologists; schools of social work were born to extend into public service sociological and psychological understanding. No extended argument should be required to establish a similar dependent relationship for journalism, architecture, pharmacy, agriculture, hotel management, education, dentistry, or public administration. The dependent professional schools are the university's instruments of public service. They fire at life point-blank. But their magazines are filled, for the firing, with ammunition provided by the garrison in the central city.

I do not wish to seem too complacent or too conventional. I am sure that men in the schools of business have been able to observe the application of theories of economics and the behavioral sciences with salutary consequences for those engaged in pursuit of pure knowledge. Important developments of a fundamental nature have been initiated in medical schools, and engineers and agronomists have performed reciprocal services of critic and judge for their more cloistered brethren of the central city. Nevertheless, it is at the core of the university that the vital spark of reflection and detached impartial speculation is fed and kept alive. If it were to die—or abandon its real mission, which is the same as to die—the outer reaches of the university would have only their own flesh on which to feed and would ultimately waste and fail as public servants. Or, if one of the professional appendages were voluntarily to sever its connection, though ever so healthy in its first proud moments of independence, it would ultimately lose its vitality.

But to preserve the present strength of this central core in the American university is not enough. It is a truism that the American achievement in engineering is fabulous. It is an equally frequent and perhaps just charge that we lack genuine originality. Our forte has remained utilitarian. We have been content to depend upon cultural imports, the Einsteins and the Fermis, for example, to provide the speculative scientific break-through. It has been enough that we see its value and exploit it. It is ominous that the scientific world, even in the international geophysical year, is no longer one world. We cannot depend on it that every speculative advance in science will be readily available to our scientific brokers. Our most important need is, therefore, cultivation of the brilliant, speculative, reflecting mind. Meeting this need is, therefore, our greatest possible service. It can be met only by strengthening the central core, in this instance the natural sciences of the university. This case has been so well argued I am almost embarrassed to restate it.

The case for the social sciences and the humanities has not been so often or so clearly stated. It should be obvious to us, however, that in half the world any speculative or original work on the needs and problems of society must and will begin from a premise so alien to us that its value to our society can be at best tangential. It should be equally transparent that, however distasteful its premise may be, the Communist community does not lack assurance and dares move with conviction toward its stated goals. We, on the other hand, are burdened with doubts and uncertainty. William Butler Yeats has stated our dilemma well in his "The Second Coming":

> The best lack all conviction
> While the worst are filled with passionate intensity.

Whether the best or not, we are those who lack conviction, and in our uncertainty and confusion we have feared and proscribed originality, thrown road blocks in the way of speculation, impugned the loyalty of anyone seeking to question or criticize our institutions, and rewarded conformity as though it were the chief virtue. There is no doubt but that we need an improved public service in the technical academic sense mentioned earlier. We desperately need understanding and enlightened public servants for our foreign missions, in state, local, and federal bureaus and in elective and appointive offices. We need them, not as a class apart, a pale image of Djilas's "New Class," but as an extension of our enlightened electorate. We need new inventive theory and/or practice in politico-economic fields that can rescue us from the absurdity of embarrassing surpluses compounded in the shelter of artificial supports. We need delivery from subsidy—whether tariff or agricultural quota.

But for social inventions congenial to the democratic premise we can afford to depend on no one but ourselves. We shall find the professional schools useful, but the detachment required for consistent original discovery, unspoiled by tendentious pressures of interest groups, is available only in the citadel at the central core of the university. We need, also, someone to interpret America to herself. In order to regain conviction we require an acquaintance with our own culture—a sympathetic knowledge of our time and place and an appreciation of the vital generalizations by which we live. For these we depend upon the philosophic, literary, and aesthetic judgments again provided only in the central city of the university. Moreover, of these something special needs be said. Congress already senses and dares support the new look required in the sciences. But no institution but the university, and no one but the academic man it supports, can be expected to understand that, unless we know ourselves, critically, but sympathetically too, we cannot recapture the cultural integrity upon which conviction depends. And without that conviction all the National Defense Education Acts in the world will be meaningless.

In these last sentences I have expressed my deepest conviction about America's present need. I believe that the university can perform its greatest possible public service by manning its central city, the sciences and humanities, with the wisest, freest minds it can find. The egghead and the ivory tower have been epithets to the utilitarian nineteenth- and twentieth-century American. They have represented to the American mind a cloistered, detached, critical, reflective, absent-minded community of speculating but impractical men. Today the theoretical, the interpretive, and the impractical have become our greatest practical need. So if you were to ask me, with due regard for economy in words, to tell what the university can do to be of the greatest possible public service, my reply would be: Eggheads, man the ivory tower.

Emergent Challenges: The State University of the Future

By Logan Wilson

I

Several years ago in an address at one of the state universities, Julian Huxley reminded his audience that man is after all a biological newcomer on this planet, and that he invented urban civilization only some five thousand years ago. He illustrated man's upstart character with a comparison given by Sir James Jeans. In the illustration, the span of time since the origin of any earthly form of life is depicted by the height of the Empire State Building. To add the proportional amount of lapsed time since the origin of civilization, a postage stamp would be stuck on the topmost point. Extending Sir James's comparison for our purposes, the millennium since the first universities were established at Salerno and Bologna would be a very thin sliver of this stamp, and the

163 years since the first student matriculated in an American state university would hardly exceed the thickness of the printer's ink on it.

And now that we are poised figuratively on a postage stamp atop the Empire State Building, let me say that this dizzying vantage point is perhaps as good as any other for a flight of fancy about the state university of the future. Before we venture into the unknown future, however, let us look briefly at the known past and make a cursory analysis of where we stand today. Despite the precarious and imperfect status of contemporary civilization, man *has* climbed a long and arduous way upward from his primordial beginnings. Higher learning has been essential to that cultural and social advancement. Neither the vastness of our cultural heritage nor the complexities of modern society would have been possible without the university. Certainly, no other institution encompasses so completely as does a great university the best that mankind everywhere has thought and said and done. No other social invention of the last thousand years has proved more useful for the discovery, conservation, and dissemination of important knowledge.

Is there another secular institution which even approaches it in epitomizing man's highest aspirations and dedication to truth and the common good? Our earliest universities, it should be remembered, were founded as places where scholars could pursue the truth, and through the ages this ideal has remained constant. Medieval centers of higher learning, however, were enclaves within a surrounding society which was largely indifferent to their purposes and not very much affected by what went on within their walls. Contemporary universities, and particularly state universities, on the other hand, are essential elements in the structure of modern society. The future of these institutions is therefore a matter of urgent concern to every citizen.

Since neither astrology nor crystal ball gazing can project the state university of the future, how does one go about the task? It seems to me that several procedures may be employed. First, we need to look at the state university as a social institution and get a broad perspective of its structure and functions. Second, we must understand the social forces in its development and the most critical factors in its present circumstances. These latter are the substantive underpinning of the first half of my topic, "Emergent Challenges." Our third procedure is to extrapolate or project the dimensions of the state university of the future.

Admittedly, none of these procedures can be followed to the satisfaction of a rigorous methodologist, and each involves more unknown variables than the one before it. Yet something of this sort must be done if we are to anticipate future needs, plan ahead to meet them, and try to avoid the dangers of having our institutions drift into the future like rudderless ships.

Our first and least difficult step, describing the structure and functions of the state university, is in itself no easy task. Like other universities, it is an institution of higher education, usually with a graduate division and one or more professional schools, licensed to confer degrees. Its principal functions are teaching, research, and public service, and in these respects it does not differ in kind from universities supported and controlled under other auspices. It cannot be sharply differentiated from other members of its genus in terms of size, scope, or quality.

What, then, are the distinguishing characteristics of the state university? The obvious differences would appear to be in support and control. For most of its support it typically depends upon legislative appropriation from tax sources rather than upon student fees, endowment income, and gifts. Its control is likewise more broadly based than in most other types of institutions. In the matter of ultimate control, nonetheless, the difference between public and private institutions is frequently exaggerated in pronouncements on the subject. As Howard Mumford Jones has pointed out, recognized academic degrees cannot be conferred anywhere in this country without governmental approval. Beginning with and ever since their colonial origins, American colleges and universities have existed as legal creatures of states, and not of churches or scholars. This is both a mere formality and a significant fact and, in Jones's opinion, explains anomalies of a theory with which the American Association of University Professors has long struggled. From time to time it "presents us with a melodrama from academic life, in which the professor is commonly cast as Eliza, the president appears as Simon Legree, and the board of regents are the baffled bloodhounds." The astonishing thing is not that such episodes occur, but that they are relatively infrequent.

Insofar as the state university is unlike comparable types of educational institutions, it differs in degree rather than kind. Being close to the needs and aspirations of the people of the state, it cannot proclaim a monolithic curriculum, be highly exclusive in its selection of students, or turn its back on applied research and other services having to do with the general public welfare. Moreover, it must compete with other state agencies and educational institutions for funds and is commonly put into a procrustean bed with them by those who determine fiscal allocations. Bureaucratic tendencies in many states result in efforts to deal with the organization of higher learning as if it could be handled like any other state agency, with the further difficulty that tax-supported colleges and universities typically share only in whatever general revenue is left after all other claims have siphoned off their predetermined portions.

Although teaching has always been a recognized basic activity, until recent years the research function has been largely a residual enterprise in all universities. Professor W. H. Cowley has noted that as late as the last decades of the nineteenth century, research had no status in the United States or in England. He cites the case in point, for example, of a famous Oxford University master who in 1890 sneered, "Research! A mere excuse for idleness; it has never achieved, and will never achieve, any results of the slightest value." What a contrast this is with the present era, when the prestige of a university tends to be gauged, in some circles at least, largely by the weight of its scholarly and scientific contributions to knowledge, both theoretical and applied.

In both its research and public service functions, the state university has less independence of choice than does the private institution. As Harlan H. Hatcher has commented, "Citizens of the state have every right to expect their university to bring all its resources in teaching, research, and public service to the solution of their problems." The heavily endowed college or university may confine itself—even though it rarely does so—to traditional forms of on-campus teaching and to whatever kinds of inquiry and other creative work its professors may choose, but "not so with state universities." Herein lies, I suspect, one of the really basic differences in the way the two types of institutions are conceived, and the chief reason for the wide panoply of activities exhibited by many state universities in the name of public service.

Suffice it to say, the concept does give rise to perils for academic freedom, to overemphases of diffused civic services at the expense of more fundamental teaching and research, and to encroachments upon the time-honored insulation of the university as an environment designed primarily for reflective thinking. Notwithstanding these defects of its virtues, the democratic ethos and pragmatic character of the American state university are among its principal claims to distinctiveness as an educational institution.

Like other types of universities, it has evolved as an instrument for preserving, systematizing, evaluating, transmitting, and enriching the cultural heritage. In common with them, it has assumed important roles in affording individual students opportunities for self-development and growth in socio-economic usefulness. Perhaps more than most other types of institutions of higher education, it has come to express the needs and aspirations of organized society and to be utilized by all the citizenry as an agency for problem solving and for facing the future. In the past, higher education, along with secondary education, may have dealt almost exclusively with the known, but the tempo of social changes makes it increasingly evident, I think, that in the future our key universities, while not abandoning any of their traditional functions, will of necessity be used more and more as instruments for coping with the uncertain and the unknown.

II

So much for a broad description of the contemporary structure and functions of the state university. What main forces are currently affecting it, and what crossroads has it reached? The most obvious and most widely discussed of these forces, of course, is the tremendous demographic upsurge. Nearly everybody now knows that the college-age population will be approximately doubled by 1970, with the strong probability of 50 per cent or more of all high school graduates continuing their formal education, as contrasted to about 30 per cent at present. There is the further likelihood that state universities may enroll a larger share of this expanded total than they now do. A second source of greater responsibility stems from the rapid growth in knowledge, the increased complexities of life in modern society, and the necessity not only for educating larger numbers but also of extending the average as well as the ablest students to ever higher levels of achievement. Third, the mounting demands for research and other services, especially from state universities, will undoubtedly be multiplied.

All of these pressures have been intensified by a spreading American realization that the adequacy of our colleges and universities is no longer merely a matter of domestic welfare to be regarded as desirable for individual and collective improvement, but as something vital to our continued existence as a free and independent nation.

If these challenges to higher education are to be met, public support and understanding must be forthcoming for an enlarged and more important role for the state university. Unfortunately, the need for greatly increased expenditures comes at a time when higher education is already heavily burdened with accumulated deficits from indifference and neglect. The financial plight of most private institutions during the period of our greatest national prosperity is generally known; less generally known is the fact that in many states legislative appropriations for higher education have similarly dwindled as a percentage of total governmental expenditures. Even a doubling of expenditures by 1970, without further inflation, will hardly enable us to hold our own, and if the exploitation of teachers and researchers is to cease, and our staffs are to be augmented by more and better minds, a major break-through is essential. (As they compare our educational and scientific potentials with those of Russia, the American public needs to know that we compensate our professors at a rate about two and a half times that paid manual laborers, whereas the Russians have a ratio of sixteen to one.)

In a free economy, however, people's attitudes rather than governmental edicts determine how much of the gross national product is to be allocated to educational enterprise. Undertakings pointed toward the general welfare and investment in future well-being must compete with expenditures for immediate consumption and personal comfort, and in this competition, the advocates of greater support for education find themselves restrained by a tradition of relying upon appeals to reason rather than organized coercion, threats of resistance, charging all the traffic will bear, and other tactics used in the market place by various economic interest groups.

While I do not underestimate the persuasiveness of the friends of higher education or the capacity of our people to meet a crisis, I think we should avoid the easy assumption that somehow all recognized needs are going to be met. In fact, I agree with Herman Wells and his Indiana associates that our most optimistic hopes are not likely to be realized; in any event, we have a present obligation to establish priorities in terms of basic needs rather than mere salability. Brain power requirements necessitate giving top priority to faculty salaries, together with an exercise of considerable restraint in the establishment of new institutions and in plant expansions of existing colleges and universities. The success of the state university in this country has already bred too many imitations, in my opinion, and legislators as well as others need to be informed that the benefits derived from monogamy are no guarantee that they would be multiplied by polygamy. I do not mean to pose any spurious antithesis between quality and quantity in higher education, but I do believe that there are limits to institutional replication and that we must choose between "protecting and re-enforcing the vitality of our enterprise even at the expense of some . . . crowding and inconvenience . . . on the one hand, and on the other, the convenience, come-one-come-all proliferating mediocrity."

In addition to the emergent challenge of adequate support and wise utilization of it, there are many critical issues having to do with public understanding. For the next few decades not all of our needs can be expressed in dollars. Above all else, the state university must be upheld and strengthened as a center of independent thought. If it is to thrive and render maximum service, it must be largely self-governing, for, as someone has said, its independence is no less essential to society than independence of the judiciary.

With increased political maturity, undue legislative interference with the state university is on the wane, but other sources of impingement appear to be pressing harder upon its autonomy. Virgil Hancher has pointed out that great decisions about its present and future are more and more being made piecemeal by individuals and agencies having no real knowledge of the issues implicit in them—yet producing a collective impact which may be staggering. I think Oliver C. Carmichael was right in asserting a few years ago that outside pressure rather than inside planning has dictated to a large extent the programs of most state universities and land-grant colleges, with other institutions affected perhaps to a lesser degree. This is not necessarily a bad thing, but the other side of the coin is that a university may suffer from under-insulation no less than from over-isolation. As the tempo of social change accelerates, society will not be able to afford to wait for popular pressures to become articulated and felt by our institutions of higher learning. More and more, our state universities will be working on frontiers of knowledge where future needs must be anticipated and even created. In short, as problem-solving agencies, our institutions will have to aid in guiding intelligently as well as reflecting faithfully a very dynamic social order.

The aims of the state university cannot be realized, nonetheless, if they are not cherished by diverse segments of society. The higher learning is not a commodity to be purchased for a stated price; for it to flourish, the people at large must believe in its importance, and must have a real respect for things of the mind and spirit. They and we must be willing to maintain the state university as the best environment we are capable of devising in which teachers and learners unite in common endeavor to pursue the truth for its own sake and to build a better society. The more we weasel over meeting the challenge, the higher the price we shall pay for our ignorance and indifference, for, as Whitehead has said,

In the conditions of modern life the rule is absolute; the race which does not value trained intelligence is doomed. Not all your heroism, not all your social charm, not all your wit, not all your victories on land or at sea, can move back the finger of fate. Today we maintain ourselves. Tomorrow science will have moved forward yet one more step, and there will be no appeal from the judgment which will be pronounced on the uneducated.

Greatly increased public understanding and support are not sufficient in themselves, nonetheless, to assure the wisest development of the future state university. We professional educators likewise need to make some hard decisions and be prepared to implement them with judicious but firm action. To begin with, we have probably oversold ourselves and the people at large on the difficulties to be surmounted when the "tidal wave" of students hits our institutions. David Henry and others have reminded us that college and university enrollments quintupled in the first twenty-five years of this century and doubled in each of the succeeding fifteen-year periods. What we have been able to do in the past, we surely can do again in the years ahead.

But in view of the many new demands upon the public purse, it seems to me that those of us associated with state universities have an obligation and an opportunity to help guide the expansion of public higher education in the direction which combines economy of effort with effectiveness of result. In my opinion, this includes the duty of aiding private institutions to increase their educational resources, and of cooperating with junior colleges, municipal institutions, and other state-supported colleges in promoting a logical division of labor to minimize wasteful rivalry and unnecessary duplication. We must acknowledge to ourselves and proclaim to others that our own state universities cannot undergo indefinite alterations in size, structure, and function without changing character and perhaps weakening their basic missions. There surely must be an optimum limit in size for a given college or university, some definable range of services it can perform best, and some educational needs which can be met more appropriately by other institutions of higher learning or outside agencies. Unless we want more statewide "super boards" to be created and more powers to be assumed by those already in existence, we educators in all sorts of colleges and universities, not to mention our friends in secondary education, had better get our heads together within the respective states and try to think these things through.

I am of the further opinion that our state universities have been more prone than any others to try to be all things to all students, and the popularity we have attained has unfortunately encouraged a host of state colleges to do likewise—unfortunately for us as well as for them. It is no wonder that many prospective students and their parents have very little basis for discriminating in making their institutional choices. In many sections of the country there has long been an intense competition among state-supported colleges and universities (not to mention others) for sheer numbers of students, and the encouragement in some quarters of a folk belief that every institution has a great deal to offer any prospective enrollee. Darley, Riesman, and others have hinted that it might be helpful to publish a consumer's guide to higher education. Just who would sponsor such a venture I do not know, but we owe it to students, parents, and our other constituents to supply them with more objective standards of value than they can get from the promotional materials many of our institutions disseminate in Chamber of Commerce style.

Moreover, I think the time has come when many state universities can serve their states best by embarking upon selective admissions and leaving to community colleges, regional institutions, and others a larger share of discharging the important democratizing role of higher education. I would agree with John Caldwell that this is feasible—and in my judgment very desirable—in a state which supports enough other institutions with liberal admission standards. If in so doing we can hold off political pressures which might be exerted on behalf of the unqualified to replicate watered-down versions of university programs elsewhere, then our state universities would all stand a better chance of becoming worthy capstones of public education. Each type of institution, in turn, would be encouraged to achieve higher standards of excellence in performing its particular functions, and all along the line students would be matched with opportunities suited to their needs and capabilities.

With more students to be taught, more to be learned, more general services to be performed, and a greater sense of urgency on all sides, we cannot continue to sanction a relatively undirected and unending proliferation of our course offerings and an unlimited piling up of the number of subjects required for graduation. And here I am not advocating a return to the medieval quadrivium, a relaxation of requirements, or a putting on of blinders to innovations. Instead, I will flatly state my view that most comprehensive universities, including my own (which, by the way, has recently trimmed many of its departmental listings), could effect an educational improvement if right now they would eliminate at least 20 per cent of the courses cluttering up their catalogues, and to the question, "Why stop at 20 per cent?" I really have no ready answer!

If quality levels are to be upheld and improved, the coherence and meaningfulness of the educational experience are to be enhanced, and the time demands of the educative process in special and professional fields are to produce graduates who are still short of middle age, better ways of teaching and learning must be utilized. Somehow, we must achieve a major break-through in educational results. Our mountainous labors with courses and degree patterns and libraries are still producing mousy consequences. Can we *teach* more? We should be able to double the distance between the mark that designates a freshman's knowledge and that which shows a senior's attainment.

Moreover, it is already clear that all together we are getting nowhere in strengthening our faculties by merely raiding one another; we shall have to find the means not only to attract many more individuals into university work as a life career, but also to induce a larger number of exceptionally able individuals into teaching and research. Ways and means will have to be devised to enable them to reach larger numbers of students with no loss in learning efficiency. And, as Dr. Cowley has stated, the three functions of general education, special education, and research must be better blended than at present.

In short, for us educators and the public this is a time for decision and action in American education and in the state university. The really big challenge to all of us is not in outer space, but in inner space —the space between the ears, as my colleague Harry Ransom has aptly put it. Manpower in this era is essentially brain power, or the intellectual resources we shall be able to muster. It is in this regard that the state university is being challenged as never before in history.

III

What the state university will be like several decades hence is anybody's guess, but extrapolating from its historical development, I think it is safer to predict evolutionary than revolutionary change. Colleges and universities are among our most stable and durable social institutions, with their unusual continuity being attributable both to their identification with lasting values and to their adaptability. Despite its viability, the state university has undergone no radical alteration in structure and function during the last quarter century, and I venture to say that its main institutional characteristics will be readily recognizable by those of us who still may be around in another quarter century.

Although the size of many of our state universities may be at least doubled by then, I doubt that there will be any appreciable number of those gargantuan institutions being forecast by a simple process of projection for nearly every metropolitan area. In fact, I am of the opinion that the largest universities, like our largest cities, may be already approaching the outer limits of effective operation on single campuses, and I anticipate that their further growth will occur on satellite or affiliated campuses. In those states where a logical division of labor is worked out in higher education, it is likely to be the community and regional colleges which will play ever more important roles in democratizing education for burgeoning numbers and in routing the abler and more ambitious of them to centers of advanced study, such as our future state universities will more and more become.

I do not mean to imply, however, that our major state universities will abandon their undergraduate divisions and relegate general education or the liberal arts to other institutions. Instead, my guess is that their lower divisions' offerings will be intended primarily for students of better-than-average ability, with the prospect that liberal education will gain rather than lose in curricular significance as it becomes better integrated than at present with special and professional education. Yet the state university will of necessity undergo its greatest instructional expansion and development in the graduate division and in its professional schools. As is already true in such fields as chemistry and physics, for example, graduate work will be a *sine qua non* for many of those who wish to pursue professional careers, and the bachelor's degree will have about the same significance that a high school diploma did some years ago. Our professional schools in turn are likely to be heavily influenced by the research emphasis of the graduate division as they emphasize experimentation and other activities intended to improve rather than merely perpetuate existing applications of knowledge.

The rapid growth in knowledge may be expected to continue and indeed to be accelerated, but I doubt that departments and courses will proliferate at the same tempo they have in the past. Less cumbersome and more economical ways of organizing subject matter in terms of fundamental concepts will be found, and ways will be devised to stress the relatedness rather than the separateness of similar fields of inquiry. All of this will not be accomplished, to be sure, without some resistance from those who cherish the benevolent anarchy which has traditionally prevailed within the university as a loose confederation of departments and schools held together, as Clark Kerr has said, mainly by one plumbing system.

Admission to the state university will become a privilege for those who have earned it rather than a right of all high school graduates. In this setting there will be more emphasis on independent learning and less on dependent teaching, with the seminar, the library, and the laboratory assuming a greater importance in the educative process. The other part of this picture, I think, is that the efficacy of various teaching methods will be much better known than at present, with a wider use of mechanical aids, such as television and other audio-visual devices, to enable the best teachers to reach larger numbers of students in those kinds of teaching where the face-to-face relationship is not essential. As these changes occur, it is to be hoped that there will be some reversal of what Dean Woodward has termed the "shift from learning and wisdom to proficiency and competence" as principal objectives of the university.

With the student body becoming less heterogeneous, the faculty, on the other hand, is likely to become more so. This paradoxical situation will result, I think, from the fact that we simply will not be able to produce enough Ph.D.'s to maintain the same minimum level of professional qualification in the future that we have in the past. In our large state universities, not to mention other kinds of institutions of ramified structure and function, "the body of equals" tradition for the faculty will necessarily go by the board as a greater range of variation in capability and responsibility has to be recognized in emoluments and other reflections of increased social differentiation. Although we may continue to pay lip-service to the uniformity of the teacher-scholar ideal for everyone, I suspect that in practice we may be forced to abandon it in the recruitment and retention of some members of our faculties. Moreover, I join with L. A. DuBridge in anticipating that, in leading universities, salaries for full professors will advance from $10,000–$15,000 levels to $20,000–$30,000 levels.

One reason our state universities are likely to become centers for advanced study and research in their respective states is that these activities will become progressively more expensive. Few states will be able to afford more than one or two such centers, and, aside from the heavy financial investments required, there will not be enough really creative scholars and scientists to spread around everywhere. Indeed, it can be argued on the basis of some recent trends toward interstate and inter-institutional schemes of cooperation in the development and maintenance of comprehensive libraries and costly laboratories that state boundary lines may have to be ignored in the development of a few outstanding centers of learning and inquiry which ought to be geographically dispersed throughout the nation.

I am willing to predict that in most parts of the country a high proportion of these centers will be state universities with greater and more diversified financial support than that of other colleges and universities. Under such a development, I believe further that these leading universities will draw more and more direct support from business, industry, and other sources than in the past. New relationships will arise, and because more voices will want to be heard in educational decision making, the need for continuous coordination and planning between the state university and other groups will become more vital. Whether this integration of effort will be voluntary or imposed will depend, of course, upon the quality of educational leadership which emerges during the next few decades. In any event, time alone will tell whether our state universities are going to be prominently represented among the necessarily limited number of centers of higher learning where the majority of our scholars, scientists, and highly trained professional workers will be educated in the future and where the advancement of knowledge will largely take place.

A by-product of the heavy costs of education and research at such centers will be the requirement of a more rational organization of the university as a social system. I think its ends or objectives will have to be more clearly defined, its means of achieving them more closely scrutinized, and its accomplishments more rigorously appraised. Since the university deals largely with intangibles and has no unitary output which can be evaluated with a simple balance sheet, it will never lend itself to such analysis as readily as does the business corporation, but I am convinced that at least some of the concepts of modern management might be more widely utilized in our colleges and universities than they now are. Doing this while simultaneously preserving the freedom and vigor of the university as a center of independent thinking, however, will necessitate the invention of special approaches not currently in use in business and industry. Notwithstanding the difficulties to be surmounted, I believe that our universities of the future will have evolved more efficient as well as more effective means of utilizing their faculty, staff, and facilities.

A corollary of this development, I predict, will be the stripping off of some services now performed by the state university for its various constituencies. Although it may be expected to perform new and even more important services for the economic interest groups of the wider community, I believe it will abandon most of its trade-school functions and essentially apprenticeship-type programs. As it discovers what it can do better than any other agency, it will forego those activities and services which can be done equally well and perhaps even better elsewhere. Its extension or adult education programs will continue to flourish and in many instances become vastly more significant than in the past, but it will leave to state departments of education, junior and community colleges, and other civic organizations those spheres of activity which are not directly related to its central endeavors. Likewise, it will turn back to business and industry the responsibility for transmitting specific techniques having a routine character and high rate of obsolescence, and which, in addition, can be learned more economically on the job by a graduate who is firmly grounded in the fundamentals of problem solving and creative thinking.

In conclusion, perhaps I should make explicit a hitherto unmentioned assumption of continuity for our society and culture. My reason for doing so is that in view of man's recently acquired capacity for mass destruction, some degree of optimism is required merely to believe that civilization will survive. Assuming that we can learn how to avoid annihilating ourselves, however, there will still be the problems of an unstable societal equilibrium. If populations continue to grow and press ever harder upon constant or diminishing natural resources, man's ingenuity will be taxed to maintain and improve his level of living. Ignorance, incompetence, and prejudice will become ever more costly to the society which tolerates them on any wide scale, and the need for highly trained and well-disciplined minds will multiply. In short, I believe that what is known as the higher learning will be increasingly recognized and respected as a necessary condition for social survival and well-being. Under such circumstances, I think we can confidently predict an enlarged and more important role for that vital educational institution, the state university.

Participants in the Conference on Issues Facing the State University

Arthur Adams, President
American Council on Education
1785 Massachusetts Avenue
Washington, D. C.

O. C. Aderhold, President
University of Georgia
Athens, Georgia

Raymond B. Allen, Chancellor
University of California
Los Angeles, California

Robbin C. Anderson, Professor
Department of Chemistry
University of Texas
Austin, Texas

Sanford S. Atwood, Provost
Cornell University
Ithaca, New York

Joseph K. Bailey, Associate Professor
Department of Management
University of Texas
Austin, Texas

W. D. Blunk, Executive Director
Seventy-Fifth Year Observance
University of Texas
Austin, Texas

David Botter
Assistant Managing Editor
Look Magazine
488 Madison Avenue
New York, New York

A. P. Brogan, Professor
Department of Philosophy
University of Texas
Austin, Texas

Paul H. Buck, Librarian
Harvard College Library
Harvard University
Cambridge, Massachusetts

J. Alton Burdine, Dean
College of Arts and Sciences
University of Texas
Austin, Texas

· 73

John T. Caldwell, President
University of Arkansas
Fayetteville, Arkansas

Oliver C. Carmichael, Consultant
Fund for the Advancement of
    Education
Biltmore Plaza Office Building
P.O. Box 5262
Biltmore, North Carolina

Donald P. Cottrell, Dean
College of Education
Ohio State University
Columbus, Ohio

W. H. Cowley
David Jacks Professor of Higher
    Education
Stanford University
Stanford, California

F. Lanier Cox, Vice-President
Administrative Services
University of Texas
Austin, Texas

G. L. Cross, President
University of Oklahoma
Norman, Oklahoma

William C. DeVane, Dean
Yale College
Yale University
New Haven, Connecticut

Ruth E. Eckert
Professor of Higher Education
University of Minnesota
Minneapolis, Minnesota

J. P. Elder, Dean
Graduate School of Arts and Sciences
Harvard University
Cambridge, Massachusetts

Clarence Faust
Ford Foundation
477 Madison Avenue
New York, New York

Ewald T. Grether, Dean
School of Business Administration
University of California
Berkeley, California

L. E. Grinter, Dean
Graduate School
University of Florida
Gainesville, Florida

W. W. Hagerty, Dean
College of Engineering
University of Texas
Austin, Texas

John A. Hannah, President
Michigan State University
East Lansing, Michigan

M. T. Harrington, President
Texas Agricultural and Mechanical
    College System
College Station, Texas

Laurence D. Haskew, Vice-President
Developmental Services
University of Texas
Austin, Texas

Harlan H. Hatcher, President
University of Michigan
Ann Arbor, Michigan

Harold L. Hazen, Dean
Graduate School
Massachusetts Institute of Technology
Cambridge, Massachusetts

David D. Henry, President
University of Illinois
Urbana, Illinois

Norris A. Hiett, Associate Dean
Division of Extension
University of Texas
Austin, Texas

G. K. Hodenfield
Education Editor
Associated Press
330 Star Building
Washington, D.C.

74 ·

G. H. Richter, Dean
Rice Institute
Houston, Texas

John Dale Russell, Director
Office of Institutional Research
Center for the Study and Development
    of Higher Education
New York University
New York, New York

Fillmore H. Sanford, Professor
Department of Psychology
University of Texas
Austin, Texas

Otis A. Singletary, Assistant Professor
Department of History
University of Texas
Austin, Texas

Kerry Smith, Executive Secretary
Association for Higher Education
National Education Association
1201 16th Street, NW
Washington, D.C.

Herman E. Spivey, Dean
Graduate School
University of Kentucky
Lexington, Kentucky

W. R. Spriegel, Professor
Department of Management
University of Texas
Austin, Texas

E. Blythe Stason, Dean
Law School
University of Michigan
Ann Arbor, Michigan

W. O. S. Sutherland, Jr., Associate
    Professor
Department of English
University of Texas
Austin, Texas

Willis M. Tate, President
Southern Methodist University
Dallas, Texas

George Waggoner, Dean
College of Liberal Arts and Sciences
University of Kansas
Lawrence, Kansas

Herman B. Wells, President
Indiana University
Bloomington, Indiana

W. G. Whaley, Dean
Graduate School
University of Texas
Austin, Texas

John Arch White, Acting Dean
College of Business Administration
University of Texas
Austin, Texas

J. D. Williams, Chancellor
University of Mississippi
University, Mississippi

Jerre S. Williams, Professor
School of Law
University of Texas
Austin, Texas

Logan Wilson, President
University of Texas
Austin, Texas

O. Meredith Wilson, President
University of Oregon
Eugene, Oregon

W. R. Woolrich, Professor
Department of Mechanical
    Engineering
University of Texas
Austin, Texas

Lloyd S. Woodburne, Dean
College of Arts and Sciences
University of Washington
Seattle, Washington

The State University

Edited by LOGAN WILSON

ADDRESSES DELIVERED AT A CONFERENCE
HELD IN THE SEVENTY-FIFTH YEAR OF
THE UNIVERSITY OF TEXAS

has been composed in eleven point and ten
point Bodoni Book, three points leaded,
with titles in Bodoni and Bodoni Italic, and
printed by letterpress on Logan Eggshell
Wove paper, manufactured by the Chilli-
cothe Paper Company. The book was published by the University of Texas Press as a
supplement to THE TEXAS QUARTERLY, Volume Two, Number Two. Clothbound copies
issued separately from THE TEXAS QUAR-
TERLY were bound in Du Pont PX cloth.
Printing and binding were done by the
Printing Division of the University of Texas.

Lightning Source UK Ltd.
Milton Keynes UK
UKOW02f0801120614

233274UK00007B/355/P